Top 100 Questions
for
Real Estate Agents

ANDREW LOVELACE

THE QUESTIONS

showing?
- How would you handle a client who is distressed about not being able to sell their property?
- How would you manage your operations during an external crisis, like a pandemic?

REAL ESTATE AGENTS

1 INTRODUCTION TO REAL ESTATE

What does the profession of a real estate agent entail?

Before we dive into the strategies, tips, and nuances that make an agent successful, it's crucial to understand the breadth and depth of what this profession entails.

The Basics: Brokerage and Sales Transactions

At its core, the role of a real estate agent involves acting as a mediator between buyers and sellers in real estate transactions. Agents list homes for sellers and guide them through the process, from setting a price to marketing the property and closing the sale. On the buyer's side, agents find properties that match their client's needs, negotiate offers, and assist throughout the purchasing process.

Consultation and Needs Analysis

A significant part of a real estate agent's job is consultative. You're not just selling properties; you're helping people make significant life decisions. This involves listening to your clients' needs and understanding their financial standing, then making recommendations that suit their specific circumstances.

Local Market Expertise

World-class agents possess in-depth knowledge of the neighborhoods they serve, from property values and market trends to local schools, public transportation, and zoning laws. This localized expertise allows you to provide invaluable advice and make well-informed decisions for your clients.

Marketing and Visibility

The modern real estate agent is also a marketing guru. From hosting open houses and virtual tours to utilizing social media platforms and online listings, an agent's role involves various promotional activities to attract buyers and sellers. In the luxury market or in highly competitive cities, this can also involve sophisticated advertising campaigns and collaborations with influencers or local businesses.

Negotiation Skills

One of the defining features of an exceptional real estate agent is expert negotiation skills. The aim is to secure the best terms and price for your client, whether they are buying or selling. This involves an understanding of both the tangible and intangible elements that could influence a transaction, from market conditions and property features to human psychology.

Legalities and Paperwork

A real estate transaction involves heaps of legal paperwork. From contracts and disclosures to inspection reports and mortgage documents, real estate agents must be comfortable dealing with legal documents. While you don't have to be a legal expert, a strong understanding of what these documents entail and the ability to explain them to your clients is crucial.

Continuing Education and Networking

Real estate is a dynamic field. Laws, technologies, and market conditions change. Continuing education, both formal and informal, is a critical aspect of a real estate career. Moreover, networking with other professionals, from mortgage lenders to interior designers and legal professionals, can offer a holistic service to your clients.

Client Relationship and Trust

Above all, being a world-class real estate agent is about building relationships. Your clients are entrusting you with one of the most significant financial decisions of their lives. Establishing trust, providing exceptional service, and demonstrating reliability can not only make you successful in a single transaction but can also result in referrals and repeated business.

So, as you embark on this journey to become a world-class real estate agent, remember that your role is multifaceted, involving not just sales but also consultation, negotiation, legal work, marketing, and most importantly, the ability to understand and fulfill the unique needs of each client.

Why do you want to become a real estate agent?

The real estate industry holds an alluring charm for many aspiring professionals. The prospect of handsome commissions, flexible working hours, and the thrill of closing deals can indeed be quite enticing. However, as with any profession, it's not devoid of challenges. It's critical to understand both sides of the coin before venturing into this field. Here are some pros and cons that will provide insights and help you decide if you truly want to become a real estate agent.

Pros

1. **Flexible Schedule:** Real estate agents often enjoy flexible working hours. Unlike a typical 9-to-5 job, agents can tailor their schedule to meet clients' needs, making it an excellent career for those who thrive outside the traditional office environment.

2. **High Earning Potential:** Real estate agents earn a percentage of the sale price of every property they sell or lease. So, the income potential is technically unlimited - the more properties you sell, the more money you make. In luxury real estate markets, a single commission can be a significant payout.

3. **Entrepreneurial Opportunities:** Being a real estate agent offers a pathway to entrepreneurship. You have the opportunity to build your own brand, create a client base, and make business decisions.

4. **Variety and Excitement:** Every day in real estate is different. From visiting new properties to meeting diverse clients, the job keeps you on your toes. This variety can make the work exciting and far from monotonous.

5. **Helping People:** At its core, real estate is a people business. There's a profound satisfaction in helping people find their dream homes or the perfect investment. You play a pivotal role in one of the most significant financial decisions of their lives.

Cons

1. **Income Instability:** While there's high earning potential, there's also a lack of income stability, especially in the early stages of your career. Unlike salaried positions, your income relies solely on closing deals. It can take time to secure your first client and close your first sale.

2. **Work-Life Balance:** Despite the flexible schedule, real estate is not a Monday to Friday job. Clients often want to see properties in the evenings or on weekends, which can infringe on personal time.

Achieving work-life balance can be challenging.
3. **Tough Competition:** The real estate industry is fiercely competitive. In popular markets, hundreds or even thousands of agents are vying for clients. Standing out from the crowd requires hard work, smart marketing, and a good reputation.
4. **Market Fluctuations:** The real estate market is influenced by economic trends. During a recession, property sales can drop, directly affecting your income. You need to be prepared to weather these periods of downturn.
5. **Continual Learning:** Laws, market trends, and technology in real estate are continually changing. To stay competitive, you need to continually update your knowledge and adapt to industry transformations.

Being a real estate agent can be both rewarding and challenging. It's a career that demands patience, persistence, and adaptability. The pros of this profession, such as potential earnings, variety, and flexibility, are attractive. But it's crucial to weigh these against the cons, such as income instability and the impact on work-life balance.

Choosing to become a real estate agent is a significant career decision. As an aspiring agent, knowing the industry's ups and downs will help you make an informed choice about this path, ensuring your career aspirations align with the realities of the job. In the end, your success will be determined by your ability to leverage the pros and navigate through the cons, with a healthy dose of passion for real estate.

How does the real estate market function?

One of the fundamental aspects that you must understand to excel in this field is how the real estate market functions. This market is an interconnected web of players and variables that dictate property prices, availability, demand, and much more. Understanding these elements will provide you with the insights needed to navigate through complex transactions, make informed decisions, and better serve your clients.

Supply and Demand
The concept of supply and demand is the bedrock of the real estate market. When the supply of available properties exceeds demand, it becomes a "buyer's market," giving buyers more negotiating power. On the other

hand, when demand outpaces supply, it becomes a "seller's market," often resulting in higher property prices. As a real estate agent, understanding which type of market you're operating in will help you advise clients on pricing strategies, negotiation tactics, and timing.

Localized Nature

Real estate markets are highly localized, even down to specific neighborhoods within a city. Different areas have their unique characteristics, such as quality of schools, crime rates, and proximity to amenities like parks or shopping, that make them more or less desirable. A deep understanding of these local variables is crucial for a world-class real estate agent. You're not just selling a home; you're selling a lifestyle and a community.

Economic Indicators

Several macroeconomic indicators, like unemployment rates, interest rates, and consumer confidence, influence the real estate market. Lower interest rates often stimulate increased demand, as mortgage loans become cheaper. High employment rates usually indicate a strong market, as more people are financially capable of purchasing property. Keeping an eye on these indicators can provide you with valuable information on market trends.

Types of Real Estate Markets

1. **Residential Market:** This market includes single-family homes, condominiums, and townhouses. As a real estate agent, you'll often be dealing with individual or family buyers and sellers, and emotional considerations often play a significant role in decision-making.
2. **Commercial Market:** This involves office buildings, retail spaces, and other business properties. Transactions in this sector often involve higher stakes, complex negotiations, and are generally more regulated.
3. **Industrial Market:** This consists of factories, warehouses, and other industrial spaces. This market has its specialized agents, as it often requires a deep understanding of zoning laws, manufacturing operations, and logistics.
4. **Raw Land Market:** This includes farmland, undeveloped land, and large tracts to be developed. Dealing in this market requires an understanding of zoning laws, land-use restrictions, and environmental conditions.

Key Players

In addition to buyers and sellers, various other professionals play a role in the real estate market. Mortgage lenders provide the necessary financing; appraisers assess the value of properties; inspectors evaluate the condition of the home; lawyers handle the legal aspects; and real estate agents like you facilitate the transaction, ensuring that all these elements come together smoothly.

Seasonal Trends

Most real estate markets exhibit some level of seasonality. In many areas, the market tends to be more active during the spring and summer months, as families prefer to move when their children are not in school. Understanding the seasonal trends in your specific market can help you advise clients on the best times to buy or sell.

The real estate market is a complex entity influenced by a myriad of factors, both micro and macro. As a future world-class real estate agent, your grasp of how this market functions will set you apart from the competition, empowering you to offer expert advice and make well-informed decisions that align with your client's goals.

What are the essential qualities of a successful real estate agent?

The journey to becoming a world-class real estate agent is multifaceted and demanding. Yet, at the core of this journey are essential qualities that equip agents with the capabilities to excel in this highly competitive field. Whether you're starting your career or looking to elevate your practice to the next level, these qualities can serve as your compass.

Communication Skills

In real estate, clear, concise, and effective communication is vital. Agents serve as the liaison between buyers and sellers, and as such, must facilitate discussions that lead to mutual understanding and beneficial agreements. This involves not just talking but also active listening to understand the needs, concerns, and priorities of each party.

Local Market Expertise

Expertise in your local market is an invaluable asset. This encompasses everything from knowing the average price of homes in various neighborhoods to understanding the local school system, public transportation, and other amenities. A deep, nuanced understanding of your market enables you to offer insights and advice that can significantly impact your client's decision-making process.

Negotiation Skills

Negotiation is an art, and mastering it can make the difference between a good deal and a great one. A skilled negotiator knows how to craft terms favorable to their client while understanding the limit to which the other party can go. This involves a mixture of psychological insight, strategic thinking, and a clear understanding of market conditions.

Integrity and Trustworthiness

The essence of the real estate business is trust. Clients are entrusting you with one of the most significant financial decisions of their lives. Honesty, integrity, and ethics should be the cornerstones of your practice. Being upfront, transparent, and genuine not only builds trust but also fosters long-term relationships that can lead to repeat business and referrals.

Adaptability

The real estate market is constantly evolving, influenced by economic indicators, technological advancements, and social trends. An adaptable agent is always learning, open to change, and ready to adopt new technologies and methods to better serve their clients.

Emotional Intelligence

Understanding and managing emotions, both your own and those of your clients, can significantly impact your effectiveness as an agent. Buying or selling a home is often an emotionally charged experience, and the ability to navigate these emotions can lead to smoother transactions and more satisfied clients.

Resilience and Persistence

In real estate, you will face rejection, challenging clients, and deals that fall through at the last moment. Resilience is the capacity to bounce back from setbacks and persist in the face of difficulties. Without this quality, the challenges of this profession can quickly become overwhelming.

Technological Savvy

Today's real estate market relies heavily on technology. From online listings to digital signatures and virtual tours, technological proficiency is no longer optional. An agent who is comfortable using various technologies will have a significant advantage in reaching a broader audience and streamlining the transaction process.

Attention to Detail

Contracts, negotiations, and even property presentations require meticulous attention to detail. Overlooking minor details can lead to significant issues down the line. Therefore, being detail-oriented can save you and your clients from future headaches.

Strong Work Ethic

Real estate is not a nine-to-five job. It demands a strong work ethic and a willingness to go above and beyond for your clients, whether that means taking late-night phone calls, working on weekends, or quickly adapting to new information or situations.

These qualities are not just checkboxes to tick off but must be ingrained in your professional demeanor. Cultivating these traits will set you on the path to becoming not just a successful real estate agent but a world-class one, capable of delivering exceptional service that exceeds client expectations.

How can continuous learning and education help your career?

One of the fundamental principles that underline success in this field is the commitment to continuous learning and education. Real estate is an ever-evolving landscape, influenced by economic shifts, technological advancements, and changing consumer behavior. Staying ahead of the curve is not just a good habit but an absolute necessity. In this question, we'll explore why continuous learning is essential and how it can profoundly improve your career as a real estate agent.

Adaptability in a Dynamic Market

Real estate is not a static field. Market conditions can change rapidly due to various factors such as economic cycles, interest rates, and even political events. An agent who is committed to continuous learning can adapt more readily to these shifts. By understanding the latest trends and market indicators, you can offer invaluable insights to your clients, thereby becoming a trusted advisor rather than just a salesperson.

Technological Competence

The role of technology in real estate is expanding at an unprecedented rate. From virtual tours to blockchain-based contracts, the way we buy and sell properties is changing. Agents who stay updated on the latest technological trends and tools can offer better services, reach a broader audience, and streamline transactions. Ignorance of these advancements will not only hamper your efficiency but also make you less competitive.

Legal Acumen

Laws and regulations surrounding real estate transactions can be complex and are often subject to change. Whether it's new zoning laws, changes in mortgage interest rates, or alterations in property tax regulations, staying educated helps you navigate the legal intricacies more effectively. This is crucial not only for your credibility but also for minimizing risks and liabilities for your clients and yourself.

Building Expertise and Specialization

The real estate market is vast, with various niches ranging from residential and commercial to industrial and luxury markets. Continuous learning allows you to specialize in specific sectors, equipping you with targeted knowledge and expertise. This specialization can be a strong selling point, making you the go-to agent for particular types of transactions.

Personal Branding and Thought Leadership

Agents who are well-versed in various aspects of real estate and continually update their knowledge often become thought leaders in the field. Writing articles, hosting webinars, or even sharing valuable insights on social media can boost your personal brand. This not only attracts more clients but also opens doors for collaborations, partnerships, and other business opportunities.

Client Satisfaction and Referrals

A well-educated agent is better equipped to meet or exceed client expectations. Your ability to provide accurate, timely, and valuable advice will significantly impact client satisfaction. Satisfied clients are more likely to refer you to their network, generating a cycle of continuous business.

Lifelong Learning as a Business Strategy

Incorporating continuous learning is not just a personal development tool but a strategic business decision. This could mean setting aside time for reading industry journals, taking online courses, attending seminars, or even pursuing higher formal education like certifications or specializations.

Continuous learning is not an optional extra; it's a core component of a successful career in real estate. It equips you with the tools to adapt, innovate, and excel, thereby positioning you as a world-class agent in this highly competitive market. Your commitment to education and self-improvement will be reflected in the quality of service you offer, enhancing both your personal brand and your bottom line.

2 MARKET RESEARCH AND KNOWLEDGE

How important is understanding local real estate markets?

Becoming a world-class real estate agent involves mastering several facets of the profession, but one area where your expertise will truly shine is your understanding of local real estate markets. As a foundational principle of a successful real estate career, it's a topic that merits special attention. In this question, let's delve into why understanding local markets is not merely beneficial but indispensable for any aspiring or experienced real estate agent.

The Local Nature of Real Estate

While real estate is often discussed in the context of national trends and average prices, the reality is that it's highly localized. Properties just a few miles apart can differ dramatically in price, amenities, and appeal. An in-depth understanding of local markets allows you to offer specialized advice that generic industry knowledge cannot match. Whether it's the future development plans for a neighborhood, the quality of local schools, or the walkability score of an area, these localized factors heavily influence property values and buyer decisions.

Strategic Pricing

One of the most critical decisions in a real estate transaction is the listing price of a property. Setting the right price requires a nuanced understanding of the local market conditions, including comparable sales, supply and demand factors, and seasonal trends. Price too high, and the property may languish on the market; too low, and you risk leaving money on the table. An agent who can accurately gauge the pulse of the local market can offer strategic pricing advice, which can be a key determinant of how quickly a property sells and at what price.

Tailored Marketing

Different neighborhoods attract different types of buyers. A downtown loft may appeal to young professionals, while a suburban home might be more suitable for families. Understanding the local market lets you tailor your marketing strategy to target the right audience. Whether it's through open houses, social media marketing, or direct mailers, the more targeted your approach, the more effective your marketing efforts will be.

Fostering Trust and Credibility

Clients rely on your expertise to guide them through one of the most significant financial decisions of their lives. When you demonstrate a deep understanding of the local market, you not only offer valuable insights but also build trust. Your advice transitions from general recommendations to tailored strategies, bolstering your credibility and the likelihood of client satisfaction.

Negotiation Leverage

Effective negotiation is often grounded in hard facts and compelling arguments. Knowing the local market inside out gives you an edge in negotiations, whether you're representing a buyer or a seller. For instance, awareness of how long similar properties have stayed on the market, or the going rate per square foot in a particular neighborhood, can serve as powerful negotiating points.

Future Planning

Real estate is as much about the future as it is about the present. Areas that are up-and-coming today could be the hot markets of tomorrow. By keeping a finger on the pulse of local developments, zoning changes, and planned infrastructure, you can provide your clients with insights into the long-term potential of a property, which adds another layer to your consultative approach.

Career Growth and Specialization

As you deepen your understanding of local markets, you may find specific niches or neighborhoods where you excel. Specializing in these areas can set you apart from competitors, allowing you to carve out a unique brand identity and reputation.

Understanding local real estate markets is not just a good-to-have skill but an essential cornerstone of a successful real estate career. It enriches every aspect of your role, from client acquisition and retention to negotiation and closing deals. Investing time and effort to master this area is investing in the future of your career, equipping you to ascend from a good agent to a world-class professional.

What techniques do you use to understand the market trends?

To flourish in the ever-evolving realm of real estate, an agent must not only comprehend the present state of the market but also anticipate its future direction. This predictive capability relies heavily on understanding market trends. In this question, we'll demystify the techniques professionals employ to decode these trends, positioning themselves for success in any market condition.

Historical Data Analysis
By comparing current market conditions to those of the past, you can detect patterns and cycles. Such data includes home sale prices, days on the market, and volume of sales over time. Platforms like Multiple Listing Services (MLS) or local real estate boards often provide comprehensive historical data.

Absorption Rate Calculation
This rate reveals how long it will take for the current inventory of homes to be sold, given the current sales pace. A high absorption rate might indicate a seller's market, whereas a low rate might hint at a buyer's market. The formula is: Absorption Rate = Number of Sales / Number of Listings.

Supply and Demand Analysis
Monitor the number of available listings against the volume of buyers. A surplus of homes with fewer buyers can lead to a drop in prices (buyer's market). Conversely, when demand exceeds supply, prices often rise (seller's market).

Interest Rate Monitoring
Interest rates have a direct impact on mortgage affordability. A rise in rates can lead to decreased purchasing power for buyers, potentially cooling the market. Conversely, drops in interest rates can stimulate activity.

Local Economic Indicators
Unemployment rates, new business developments, and other economic indicators in a region can significantly influence real estate demand. A thriving local economy can bolster real estate prices, whereas economic

downturns can have the opposite effect.

New Construction and Development Data
A sudden surge in new construction projects might indicate optimism in the market. It's essential to gauge not only the quantity but also the types of units being constructed (e.g., luxury condos, townhomes, single-family residences).

Rental Market Trends
While distinct from the buying market, rental trends can offer insights. For instance, rising rental prices might push more individuals to consider buying.

Consumer Sentiment Surveys
Periodically, institutions and associations conduct surveys to gauge consumer sentiment regarding real estate. High optimism levels might signal an upward trend, whereas prevalent skepticism could hint at a downturn.

Government Policies and Regulations
Stay updated on local, state, and federal policies that could influence real estate, from tax incentives for first-time homebuyers to zoning law changes.

Technological Trends
Emerging technologies can reshape buyer habits, market outreach, and even property values. For instance, the rise of remote work could boost demand in suburban or rural areas over urban cores.

1Networking and Collaboration
Regular interactions with fellow agents, brokers, and other professionals in the field can provide ground-level insights. They might share observations, success strategies, or market challenges they're encountering.

1Expert Opinions and Forecast Reports
Real estate experts and organizations frequently release forecast reports, diving deep into market analysis and predictions. While these shouldn't be your sole source of information, they can offer valuable macro-level insights.

1Local Events and Changes
Always keep an ear to the ground for local events, whether they're infrastructure projects, corporate moves, or educational developments. A new school or a major company establishing headquarters in an area can be

game-changers for property demand.

Understanding market trends is a multifaceted endeavor. It's an amalgamation of data-driven insights, on-the-ground observations, and strategic forward-thinking. By incorporating these techniques into your regular practice, you'll not only deepen your understanding of the present market but also cultivate a visionary perspective, a hallmark of a world-class real estate agent.

How do I analyze a real estate market?

As you venture further into the exciting world of real estate, one of the most vital skills to master is market analysis. An in-depth understanding of your market will arm you with the insights needed to make informed decisions for both you and your clients. Here, we'll discuss a structured approach to conducting a thorough analysis of a real estate market.

Gather Basic Economic Data
Begin by obtaining a snapshot of the broader economic context in which your real estate market operates. Key metrics include employment rates, median income, population growth, and other economic indicators. Websites like the U.S. Census Bureau, local government sites, and economic development agencies often provide this information.

Real Estate Market Indicators
Collect data on key real estate indicators:
- **Home Prices**: Average and median selling prices.
- **Inventory Levels**: Number of homes listed for sale.
- **Sales Velocity**: Average time a property stays on the market.
- **Rental Yields**: If applicable, average rent and occupancy rates.

Sources can include the Multiple Listing Service (MLS), local real estate boards, and property websites.

Absorption Rates
Calculate the absorption rate, which indicates how many months it will take to sell the existing inventory at the current rate of sales. The formula is: Absorption Rate=Total Listings / Listings Sold Per Month.

Supply and Demand Trends
Keep an eye on the balance between the number of buyers and the available

inventory. A high demand with low supply typically drives up prices, signaling a seller's market. The reverse usually suggests a buyer's market.

Construction and Development Activity

Examine building permits, zoning applications, and other public records to gauge the level of new construction. New developments can indicate market optimism but also pose risks of oversupply.

Interest Rates

Monitor mortgage rates and lending trends. High rates may discourage buying, leading to a slower market, while low rates often spur buying activity.

Local Amenities and Factors

Local schools, public transport, safety, and other amenities can heavily influence property values. Websites like GreatSchools.org, WalkScore, and local police departments can provide valuable data.

Competitive Analysis

Study your competitors in the area, looking at their listing prices, marketing strategies, and customer reviews. Identify gaps in the market and areas where you can add value.

Consumer Behavior and Sentiment

Pay attention to changing preferences and behaviors among homebuyers and renters. Are people looking for larger homes due to remote work, or are they downsizing to save costs? Various surveys, social media trends, and open-house interactions can offer insights.

Historical Data Trends

Analyze how current data compares to past trends. Is the market hotter or colder than the same period last year? What cyclical patterns can you identify?

1Consult Experts and Network

Engage with local experts, attend real estate meetings, and read reports by market analysts to complement your own findings.

1Utilize Technology

Sophisticated software can help you sort and analyze data, generate reports, and even project future trends. Platforms like Zillow, Redfin, and various real estate analytics software offer powerful tools for market analysis.

1SWOT Analysis

Finally, perform a SWOT (Strengths, Weaknesses, Opportunities, Threats) analysis on your findings. This will help you understand where you can leverage your strengths, improve weaknesses, capitalize on opportunities, and mitigate threats.

Analyzing a real estate market is not a one-time task but an ongoing process. Regularly update your data and adapt your strategies to remain agile and informed. Mastering market analysis not only makes you a better advisor to your clients but also gives you a competitive edge in the dynamic landscape of real estate. Armed with data-driven insights, you'll be well on your way to becoming a world-class real estate agent.

How do you stay updated on changes in real estate laws and regulations?

In the multifaceted career of real estate, laws and regulations form an integral backdrop against which all activities unfold. Keeping abreast of changes in this domain is essential for several reasons, including compliance, informed client advice, and your own professional development. In this question, we'll explore strategies for staying updated on real estate laws and regulations.

Join Professional Associations

Organizations like the National Association of Realtors (NAR), local real estate boards, or other state-level associations often provide updates and summaries of legislative changes affecting real estate. These institutions act as advocates for real estate professionals and offer extensive resources, from newsletters to training sessions, focusing on regulatory aspects.

Sign up for Newsletters

Many legal firms and professional agencies specialize in real estate law. Subscribing to their newsletters can provide you with timely insights into any upcoming changes. Similarly, real estate-focused publications often cover legislative adjustments as part of their regular content.

Continuing Education

Most states require real estate agents to complete continuing education courses for license renewal. Take advantage of this by choosing courses that focus on legal updates or emerging trends in real estate law.

Webinars and Online Courses

Apart from mandatory continuing education, many online platforms offer courses focusing on real estate laws and regulations. Webinars are also an effective way to get real-time updates from experts in the field. Make it a habit to attend these virtual events regularly.

Networking

Networking events provide a forum to share and receive industry updates. Engage with colleagues, mentors, and professionals from related fields like real estate law, mortgage brokerage, and property management. These contacts can become invaluable sources of timely information.

Social Media and Blogs

Follow key influencers, professional organizations, and agencies in the real estate law domain on social media platforms like LinkedIn, Twitter, and Instagram. Many professionals use these channels to share updates, articles, and perspectives on legislative changes.

Legal Consultation

If your practice deals with complex transactions or you're entering uncharted territory, such as a new type of real estate investment, consulting a legal professional can be beneficial. They can provide a detailed explanation of applicable laws and upcoming changes that may affect your business.

Local Government Websites and Publications

Municipal and state websites usually publish bulletins, reports, and press releases announcing changes in local laws, including those related to real estate. Make it a routine to scan these sources for any new updates.

Internal Company Communications

If you are part of a larger real estate firm, internal communications like emails, meetings, or bulletins are likely to cover important updates on laws and regulations. Be proactive in reading and participating in such communications.

Setting Alerts

Use online alert services, such as Google Alerts, to receive updates on specific keywords like "real estate laws," "property regulations," or more localized terms that pertain to your market.

1Peer Groups and Online Forums

Joining real estate-focused peer groups and online forums can be a good way to stay informed. These platforms often feature discussions on various aspects of the profession, including changes in laws and regulations.

Staying updated on real estate laws and regulations is an ongoing process that requires a disciplined, multi-pronged approach. The real estate landscape is dynamic, with rules that evolve to match the complexities of the market. By making it a priority to stay informed, you not only protect yourself from inadvertent violations but also fortify your position as a trusted, knowledgeable advisor to your clients. This diligence, in turn, enriches your path to becoming a world-class real estate agent.

What are the essential sources for quality information in real estate?

In the fast-paced world of real estate, information is gold. To maintain a competitive edge and serve your clients effectively, it's crucial to constantly update your knowledge. The internet is a sea of data, but knowing where to fish for relevant, reliable information can make all the difference. In this question, we will discuss the essential sources that can help you stay informed and ahead in your real estate career.

Professional Associations

Organizations like the National Association of Realtors (NAR), the Urban Land Institute (ULI), and state or local real estate associations provide valuable insights through reports, publications, and training events. Membership often grants you access to exclusive data and networking opportunities.

Industry Journals and Magazines

Publications such as "Realtor Magazine," "Inman," "Property Week," and "The Real Deal" offer deep dives into various aspects of the real estate industry, including market trends, legal updates, and success stories. Their digital counterparts often provide even more timely updates.

Scholarly Articles and Research Papers

For an in-depth understanding of specific topics, look to academic journals related to real estate, urban planning, and economics. Websites like JSTOR,

Google Scholar, and specialized academic journals can provide rigorous analyses and insights.

Government Reports and Statistics

Resources like the U.S. Census Bureau, the Bureau of Labor Statistics, and the Department of Housing and Urban Development offer valuable, accurate information ranging from housing statistics to economic indicators. Local government websites may also publish studies and reports related to regional markets.

Financial News Outlets

Mainstream financial publications like "The Wall Street Journal," "Financial Times," and "Bloomberg" frequently cover the real estate market, offering a more macroeconomic perspective. These sources are particularly useful for understanding the financial aspects of real estate, such as interest rates and investment trends.

Real Estate Analytics Platforms

Websites like Zillow, Redfin, and Trulia not only list properties but also offer market analyses, trend reports, and local information. Other specialized tools like CoStar, MLS, and local property appraisers provide data that can help in market analyses.

Blogs and Podcasts

Real estate blogs like "BiggerPockets" and podcasts such as "Real Estate Coaching Radio" or "The Real Estate Guys" provide more casual yet insightful perspectives. They can be an excellent way to absorb information during commutes or downtime.

Social Media and Forums

Platforms like LinkedIn and Twitter offer a wealth of information when you follow industry leaders, hashtags, or specialized real estate groups. Online forums like Reddit's r/RealEstate can also provide a grassroots view of current trends and issues.

Networking Events and Conferences

While not a 'source' in the traditional sense, the importance of direct interpersonal exchanges of information cannot be overstated. Conferences, seminars, and industry-specific events offer not just knowledge but also the opportunity for real-time interaction with experts.

Books and Ebooks

Don't underestimate the power of a well-written book on real estate fundamentals, strategies, or market analysis. Both traditional and electronic books can provide timeless insights.

Consulting with Experts

Sometimes the best source of information is a one-on-one consultation with an industry expert. This could be a mentor, a seasoned real estate investor, or professionals like lawyers or accountants who specialize in real estate.

Local Community Resources

Local newspapers, community boards, and small-scale events often provide information that larger sources may overlook. These can include things like upcoming local legislation affecting property taxes, or news on local developments.

As a real estate agent, your ability to sift through and analyze information effectively directly impacts your success. Whether you are seeking information on laws, market trends, property values, or client behavior, each source offers its unique benefits. Balancing a variety of sources can help you create a rounded, well-informed view of the real estate landscape, setting you on the path to becoming a world-class real estate agent.

How do you evaluate a property's value?

In the world of real estate, determining a property's value is perhaps one of the most crucial skills you can master. Whether you're working with buyers or sellers, a precise valuation can help in negotiations, listing prices, or deciding on a fair offer. So, how do you accurately evaluate a property's value? This question offers you an in-depth look at the methods and factors you should consider.

Comparative Market Analysis (CMA)

The Comparative Market Analysis is the cornerstone of property valuation for real estate agents. This involves examining the sale prices of similar properties ("comps") in the same area, ideally sold within the last six months. While no two properties are exactly alike, look for comps with similar features such as square footage, the number of bedrooms and bathrooms, and other amenities.

Price per Square Foot

Another simple yet effective method is calculating the price per square foot of the comps and then applying it to the subject property. This gives you a ballpark figure that can be refined using other methods.

Online Valuation Tools
Online tools like Zillow's Zestimate can provide an initial estimate, but remember that these are generated via algorithms that may not account for the unique characteristics of a property or the local market conditions. They are good starting points but should be corroborated with other methods.

Local Market Conditions
Is it a buyer's or a seller's market? Market conditions play a critical role in property valuation. For instance, in a seller's market, properties may be valued higher due to increased demand, and vice versa.

Property Condition and Upgrades
A property that's recently been renovated or has high-end appliances and finishes will naturally fetch a higher price. Inspect the property thoroughly to evaluate its condition. Keep an eye out for both structural and aesthetic details.

Location, Location, Location
The neighborhood's desirability is a significant influence on property value. Proximity to amenities, quality of local schools, crime rates, and future developments can all impact a home's market value.

Economic Indicators
Interest rates, employment rates, and the overall health of the economy can impact property values. Be aware of broader economic conditions and how they might affect the local real estate market.

Appraisal
A professional appraisal is often the final word in property valuation, especially for mortgage approval. However, an appraiser's report can also offer insights into how they arrived at a particular valuation, providing you with useful criteria for your own assessments.

Tax Assessments
While often less accurate than other methods, reviewing tax assessments can provide some valuation clues, especially when it comes to assessing land value and improvement value separately.

Revenue Generation Potential

For investment properties, consider the income approach, which focuses on the potential revenue the property could generate. This often involves calculating the capitalization rate, which is the expected annual income of the property divided by its current market value.

Consult with Colleagues

Sometimes, the best insight comes from sharing data and perspectives with colleagues who have extensive experience in the local market.

Intuition and Experience

As you gain experience, your own intuition for assessing a property's value will improve. Always remember, however, that intuition is most effective when backed by solid data.

Valuing a property is both an art and a science, requiring a combination of analytical skills, local market understanding, and sometimes even a bit of intuition. Each method of evaluation offers its own insight, and combining multiple methods provides the most accurate estimate. Mastering this vital skill sets you on the path to becoming a world-class real estate agent, capable of serving your clients with expertise and confidence.

3 NETWORKING AND RELATIONSHIPS

How do you build your network as a real estate agent?

As a real estate agent, one of the most crucial aspects of your success lies in your ability to build, nurture, and expand your network. A strong professional network can provide a steady stream of referrals, advice, and support that will help you to achieve your career goals. This section will explore several strategies that will help you to effectively build your network as a real estate agent.

Start with Your Immediate Circle
The first step towards building your network is to start with the people you already know. Your friends, family, and acquaintances can be a great source of referrals and introductions. Make sure they all know that you are a real estate agent and what kind of properties you specialize in. Also, ask them to refer you to anyone they know who might be interested in buying or selling a property.

Attend Networking Events
Attending networking events is another effective way to expand your network. These events could be real estate-specific, such as open houses, conferences, and seminars, or they could be more general networking events, like local business meetups. When you attend these events, remember to be proactive and approachable. Don't just hand out your business cards; engage in meaningful conversations, ask questions, and show genuine interest in other people's work.

Build Online Presence
In this digital age, having a strong online presence is absolutely essential. This includes having a professional website, being active on social media, and maintaining a presence on real estate listing sites. Sharing valuable

content related to real estate, such as market trends, tips for buyers and sellers, and showcasing your listings can position you as a knowledgeable professional. It can also attract potential clients and connections to you.

Join Professional Associations

Joining professional associations related to real estate can provide you with numerous networking opportunities. Associations often hold gatherings and events that can help you connect with other professionals in your field. Additionally, these associations can give you access to resources and training that can help you improve your skills and knowledge.

Volunteer in Your Community

Volunteering in your community not only allows you to give back, but it also helps you to meet people and make connections. Whether it's a local charity event, a community clean-up, or a neighborhood association meeting, being involved in your community can greatly broaden your network and increase your visibility.

Foster Relationships with Other Professionals

Building relationships with other professionals such as mortgage brokers, home inspectors, interior designers, and attorneys can also greatly enhance your network. These professionals can not only provide you with referrals but can also offer valuable advice and information that can help you serve your clients better.

Follow Up

Building a network is not just about making new connections; it's also about maintaining and nurturing those connections. This means following up with people after you meet them, keeping in touch regularly, and providing help and support whenever you can. A strong network is built on mutual support and trust, so always strive to be helpful and reliable.

Building a robust network as a real estate agent involves a combination of strategies. It requires you to be proactive, approachable, and genuinely interested in others. It also requires persistence and consistency. Remember, networking is not a one-time event, but a continuous process that should be an integral part of your career as a real estate agent. With a strong network, you will have a powerful tool that can greatly contribute to your success in the competitive world of real estate.

How important are interpersonal skills in this profession?

Interpersonal skills, often referred to as people skills, are crucial to most professions. This is especially true in the real estate industry, a business grounded in human interaction and relationship building. As a real estate agent, your success is determined not only by your knowledge of the market or your skill in negotiation, but also by your ability to connect with people on a personal level. Interpersonal skills are the bedrock upon which successful real estate careers are built.

Firstly, let's understand what we mean by interpersonal skills. These are abilities that facilitate interaction and communication with others. They include effective listening, clear articulation of ideas, empathy, patience, problem-solving, and the ability to read and respond to the emotions of others. In the context of real estate, these skills are used in every single interaction, from initial meetings with clients to closing sales.

One of the primary reasons interpersonal skills are so important in real estate is that buying or selling a property is often an emotionally charged process for clients. They might be purchasing their first home, selling the house they raised their children in, or facing financial hardship. As a real estate agent, you need to be able to navigate these emotional waters, offering support, understanding, and guidance. This requires excellent interpersonal skills.

Negotiation, a key aspect of real estate transactions, also heavily relies on interpersonal skills. A successful negotiator must be able to understand the needs and wants of both parties, facilitate open and productive communication, and find a compromise that satisfies all. They need to be assertive without being aggressive, persuasive without being manipulative. This delicate balance is achieved through advanced interpersonal skills.

Furthermore, real estate is a referral-based business. Happy clients refer their friends, family, and colleagues to their trusted real estate agent. The ability to establish and maintain positive relationships with clients is therefore essential. Clients won't recommend you solely based on the fact that you helped them find a house or sell their property. They will recommend you because of the way you made them feel throughout the process. Did you listen to their needs? Were you patient and understanding? Did you communicate effectively? All of these factors play into a client's overall satisfaction and willingness to refer you to others.

It's also important to note that real estate is an industry where networking plays a significant role. It's not just about the relationships you build with your clients but also with other professionals in the field. These include mortgage brokers, home inspectors, appraisers, and other real estate agents. Building a wide and diverse professional network can open up opportunities and provide valuable insights into the market, and this requires solid interpersonal skills.

Interpersonal skills are absolutely critical in the real estate industry. They enable you to build strong relationships with clients and other professionals, navigate the emotional aspects of buying and selling property, and negotiate successful deals. They are as important, if not more so, as understanding market trends or real estate law. So, if you're looking to become a successful real estate agent, start by honing your interpersonal skills. The investment will pay off in a rewarding and successful career.

In the following questions, we will delve into how to develop these skills and use them effectively in your real estate career. We will provide practical strategies and tips, real-life scenarios, and expert insights to help you become a world-class real estate agent.

How do you handle difficult clients?

One of the most challenging aspects of working in real estate is managing difficult clients. These clients can be demanding, irritable, indecisive, or even disrespectful. However, it's essential to remember that your job as a real estate agent is to serve your clients, no matter how challenging. This section will provide you with strategies and techniques to effectively handle difficult clients and maintain your professionalism.

First of all, always maintain an attitude of empathy. Keep in mind that buying or selling a property is often an emotional process for clients, and these emotions can sometimes manifest as difficult behavior. Empathy allows you to understand where the client is coming from, which can help guide your interactions with them. Listen to their concerns, validate their feelings, and assure them that you are there to help them achieve their real estate goals.

Next, establish clear boundaries. While it's important to be available and responsive to your clients, you also need to set limits to protect your own time and energy. Let your clients know your working hours and how they can best communicate with you. Setting these boundaries at the onset of your relationship can prevent misunderstandings and frustrations further down the line.

Communication is key when dealing with difficult clients. Always strive to be clear, concise, and transparent in your interactions. Avoid using jargon or industry-specific terms that your client might not understand. Instead, break down complex information into manageable pieces. Regular updates are also crucial. Even if there's no significant progress in their transaction, a quick check-in can reassure them that you're actively working on their case.

Problem-solving is another critical skill in managing difficult clients. If a client is unhappy, find out what the issue is, and come up with possible solutions. You might not always be able to fix the problem completely, but showing your client that you're willing to take steps to address their concerns can go a long way in building trust and mitigating difficult behavior.

In some situations, a client may become irrationally difficult or even abusive. In these cases, it's important to stay calm and composed. Do not respond with anger or frustration, no matter how provoked you may feel. If necessary, take a moment to collect yourself before responding. Always respond in a professional manner and try to redirect the conversation back to the task at hand.

Lastly, remember to take care of yourself. Dealing with difficult clients can be stressful and emotionally draining. Make sure to take breaks when needed, practice stress management techniques, and seek support from colleagues or mentors. You can't effectively serve your clients if you're burned out or overwhelmed.

Handling difficult clients is undoubtedly challenging, but it's also an essential part of being a real estate agent. By demonstrating empathy, establishing boundaries, communicating effectively, problem-solving, staying composed, and practicing self-care, you can successfully navigate these challenging situations. Remember, every difficult client is an opportunity for growth and learning. By honing your skills in dealing with difficult clients, you'll be well on your way to becoming a world-class real estate agent.

How do you maintain good relationships with other real estate professionals?

As a real estate agent, building and maintaining a professional network is crucial to your success. This network includes not only your clients but also other real estate professionals. These relationships can provide referrals, advice, and support, all of which can help you become a world-class agent. In this question, we will explore strategies to maintain good relationships with other real estate professionals.

Respect and Professionalism

The first rule of maintaining good relationships is to treat everyone with respect and professionalism. This includes your peers, competitors, and everyone in between. Remember, the real estate industry is a small world, and your reputation is your most valuable asset. Always conduct yourself in a manner that reflects well on you and your profession.

Communication

Good communication is the backbone of any successful relationship. Keep your lines of communication open and always be responsive. When you receive inquiries, referrals, or feedback, respond promptly and professionally. Show appreciation for the help you receive and always give credit where it's due.

Collaboration

Collaboration is key in the world of real estate. You'll often find that you can accomplish more by working together with other professionals than you can on your own. Whether you're co-listing a property, sharing market information, or teaming up for a marketing event, always strive for a win-win situation.

Networking

Networking is not just about attending events and handing out business cards. It's about building meaningful relationships. When you meet new people, take the time to get to know them. Show genuine interest in what they do and offer your assistance where you can. Remember, networking is a two-way street.

Education and Training

Keep up to date with the latest industry trends and regulations. Attend seminars, workshops, and conferences. This will not only enhance your knowledge but also provide opportunities to interact with other professionals. Sharing insights and experiences with your peers can build stronger relationships.

Mentorship

Mentoring and being mentored are great ways to build relationships. If you're a seasoned agent, consider mentoring a new agent. You will not only help guide someone else's career, but you'll also learn new things and gain a fresh perspective. If you're new to the industry, seek out a mentor who can help you navigate the complexities of the real estate world.

Reciprocity

Remember the principle of give and take. If you want referrals from other agents, you need to be willing to give referrals as well. If you've received advice or assistance, look for ways to return the favor.

Conflict Resolution

Conflicts are inevitable in any profession. When they arise, address them directly and professionally. Avoid personal attacks and focus on the issue at hand. Seek to understand the other person's viewpoint and work towards a resolution that's acceptable to both parties.

Social Interaction

Don't limit your interactions to purely professional settings. Engage with your peers in social settings too. Attend industry events, join real estate clubs, and participate in community activities. These can help build rapport and foster stronger relationships.

Ethical Behavior

Maintain high ethical standards in all your interactions. Be honest, transparent, and fair. Abide by the rules and regulations of your profession and respect the rights of others.

Maintaining good relationships with other real estate professionals is a vital aspect of being a successful real estate agent. By respecting and supporting each other, you can create a professional environment that benefits everyone involved. Remember, in real estate, your network is your net worth.

What role does a mentor play in a real estate agent's success?

A mentor, often an experienced and successful real estate agent, plays an invaluable role in the professional development and success of a novice real estate agent. The real estate industry can be a complex, challenging, and competitive field. Having someone who has navigated these waters successfully and is willing to share their wisdom, experience, and contacts can make a significant difference in a new agent's career trajectory.

One of the most crucial roles a mentor plays is imparting tacit knowledge. This involves nuances of the industry that aren't typically covered in training programs or textbooks but are learned through years of practical experience. It could range from understanding the local market trends, dealing with difficult clients, to navigating through complex transactions. This shared knowledge can help a new agent avoid common pitfalls and shorten their learning curve.

Apart from sharing knowledge, mentors also provide emotional support and act as a sounding board. Real estate can be a high-stress career, with its constant pressure to meet targets, dealing with clients' expectations, and navigating through volatile markets. Having a mentor to turn to during stressful situations or when faced with difficult decisions can provide a sense of reassurance and stability. They can offer perspective, advice, or simply a sympathetic ear during challenging times.

Mentors can also help build professional networks. Networking is a critical aspect of real estate; it's not just about what you know, but who you know. A mentor with a well-established network can introduce a new agent to potential clients, industry professionals, and other valuable contacts. These introductions can lead to partnerships, deals, and opportunities that might not have been accessible otherwise.

Moreover, mentors often challenge their mentees to reach their full potential. They can identify strengths that the mentee may be unaware of and encourage them to leverage these strengths. Similarly, they can pinpoint weaknesses or areas of improvement that the mentee needs to work on. This objective feedback is vital for personal and professional growth.

Furthermore, mentors can serve as role models, demonstrating what a successful real estate career looks like. By observing their mentor, a new agent can learn about professional ethics, effective negotiation techniques, client service excellence, and other qualities that contribute to success in the industry.

Lastly, a good mentor fosters a sense of accountability. They set expectations and monitor progress, pushing their mentees to achieve their goals. This can be particularly beneficial in the early stages of a real estate career when motivation may wane in the face of obstacles or slow progress.

A mentor plays a pivotal role in a real estate agent's success. They provide guidance, emotional support, networking opportunities, constructive feedback, and a model of success to aspire towards. They challenge and push their mentees to continually learn, grow, and achieve their goals.

However, it's important to remember that the benefits of mentorship are not one-sided. Mentors also benefit by enhancing their leadership skills, gaining new perspectives, and deriving satisfaction from helping others succeed. Therefore, mentorship is a mutually beneficial relationship that contributes to the overall success and growth of the real estate industry.

So, if you're embarking on a career in real estate, seek out mentorship opportunities. And if you're an experienced agent, consider offering your wisdom and experience to those just starting in the field. After all, the essence of real estate is not just about properties and transactions, but about people and relationships.

4 SALES AND MARKETING

How do you differentiate yourself in a competitive market?

In the dynamic world of real estate, standing out from the crowd is more than just a desirable trait; it is a necessity. With countless agents vying for the same business, it's crucial that you differentiate yourself to attract and retain clients. This question will provide you with practical strategies to distinguish yourself in a competitive real estate market.

Define Your Unique Selling Proposition (USP)

Your USP is what sets you apart from other real estate agents. It can be your specialized knowledge in a specific type of property, your exceptional negotiation skills, or your unrivaled network of contacts. Whatever it is, your USP should be the core message of your branding efforts. It's the answer to the question, "why should a client choose you over another agent?"

Cultivate a Personal Brand

Establishing a personal brand is an effective way to differentiate yourself. A personal brand is essentially your reputation; it's what people say about you when you're not in the room. It encompasses your values, your style, your expertise, and your unique approach to real estate. Your brand should permeate every aspect of your work, from your marketing materials to the way you communicate with clients.

Master Social Media Marketing

Leveraging social media allows you to connect with prospective clients on a personal level. Sharing valuable content on platforms such as Facebook, LinkedIn, Twitter, and Instagram can help you stand out in the digital space. But remember, it's not just about posting listings. Share market insights, offer home buying or selling tips, showcase your knowledge of the local area, and engage with your followers to build relationships and credibility.

Provide Exceptional Customer Service

In a competitive market, providing superior customer service can give you a significant edge. This involves understanding and anticipating your clients' needs, being responsive and accessible, and going above and beyond to ensure their satisfaction. Remember, a satisfied client can become a repeat client and may also refer you to their network.

Become a Neighborhood Expert

Becoming a neighborhood expert can significantly differentiate you from other agents. This means having in-depth knowledge of the local market, including pricing trends, neighborhood amenities, school districts, and future developments. Clients often value agents who can provide them with comprehensive information about the community they're interested in.

Continual Learning

Real estate is a dynamic field, and what worked yesterday may not work today. Continual learning is therefore crucial to stay ahead of the competition. Attend industry seminars, participate in webinars, read widely, and stay abreast of the latest market trends and technological advancements.

Build Strategic Partnerships

Partnerships with local businesses, lenders, contractors, or other real estate professionals can help you provide a broader range of services to your clients. These partnerships can not only extend your network but also provide additional value to your clients, further setting you apart from the competition.

Differentiating yourself in a competitive real estate market involves more than just selling properties. It requires defining your unique selling proposition, cultivating a personal brand, mastering social media marketing, providing exceptional customer service, becoming a neighborhood expert, committing to continual learning, and building strategic partnerships. By implementing these strategies, you'll be on your way to becoming a world-class real estate agent.

How do you market a property to attract potential buyers?

Marketing a property effectively is an essential skill in the real estate industry. It can mean the difference between a property that lingers on the market for months and one that is snapped up immediately. In this question, we will delve into the techniques and strategies that can help you attract potential buyers and maximize the property's value.

Firstly, it is important to understand your target market. Who is the property most likely to appeal to? Is it a family home, a starter home for a young professional, a retirement property, or an investment opportunity? Once you have identified your target market, you can tailor your marketing efforts to appeal to them directly.

Next, you need to highlight the property's unique selling points (USPs). What sets this property apart from the others in the neighborhood? It could be anything from an updated kitchen, a spacious backyard, proximity to good schools or local amenities, or a stunning view. Use professional-quality photos and videos to showcase these USPs. In the digital age, the majority of potential buyers will see the property online before they visit in person. Therefore, high-quality visuals are crucial to making a good first impression.
Virtual tours are another excellent way to attract potential buyers. They allow potential buyers to explore the property from the comfort of their own homes, giving them a sense of the layout and space. This can be an especially useful tool when marketing to out-of-town buyers.

Your property description should not only list the features of the property but also evoke an image of the lifestyle the property offers. Instead of simply stating "three-bedroom, two-bathroom house with a large garden," you might say, "Family-friendly three-bedroom home with plenty of space for the kids to play in the secure, private garden." The goal is to help potential buyers visualize themselves living in the property.

Social media is a powerful marketing tool that should not be overlooked. Platforms such as Facebook, Instagram, and LinkedIn allow you to reach a large audience. You can use these platforms to share photos, videos, virtual tours, and any other promotional materials you have created for the property.
Don't forget the power of traditional marketing methods. 'For Sale' signs, direct mail campaigns, and local press advertisements can still be effective, particularly for attracting local buyers. Networking with other local agents can also be beneficial, as they may have clients who are looking for a property just like yours.

Open houses are another tried-and-true method of attracting potential buyers. They give people the chance to explore the property in their own time and imagine themselves living there. Staging the property for the open house can help create a welcoming and appealing atmosphere. Remember, you're not just selling a property; you're selling a lifestyle.

Finally, remember that communication is key. Respond promptly to inquiries and be ready to provide additional information or arrange viewings at short notice. The more accessible and accommodating you are, the more potential buyers you will attract.

Marketing a property effectively requires a deep understanding of your target market, a comprehensive multi-channel marketing strategy, and exceptional communication skills. By honing these skills, you will be on your way to becoming a world-class real estate agent.

What's your strategy for handling objections and rejections?

Being a successful real estate agent is not just about finding excellent properties and presenting them to potential buyers. It's also about how you handle objections and rejections, which are inevitable in this industry. It's crucial to have a solid strategy in place to manage these situations effectively, and that is what we will explore in this question.

Firstly, it's important to understand that objections and rejections are a part of the sales process. They are not a reflection of your skills or abilities; instead, they are a sign that the client needs more information or reassurance before making a decision. Therefore, when you face objections, view them as opportunities to provide additional value and clarify any concerns the client may have.

The first step in handling objections is to listen carefully. Resist the temptation to immediately jump in and respond. Instead, let the client express their concerns fully. This will not only help you understand their needs better, but it will also demonstrate that you respect their opinions and value their input.

Once you have understood the objection, the next step is to empathize. Put yourself in the client's shoes and try to see things from their perspective. This will help you address their concerns more effectively. For instance, if the client is worried about the property's price, instead of immediately defending your valuation, you could say something like, "I understand that the price is a significant factor in your decision. Let's look at comparable properties in the area and discuss why this property is priced as it is."

After empathizing, it's time to respond. Use the information you've gathered to address the client's concerns directly and honestly. If you don't know the answer, don't bluff. Instead, assure the client that you will find the answer and get back to them. Remember, your credibility is on the line, so honesty is always the best policy.

Rejections, on the other hand, can be a bit more challenging to handle. However, they also offer learning opportunities. If a deal falls through or a client decides to work with another agent, ask for feedback. Understanding why they chose not to work with you can provide valuable insights into how you can improve your approach and become more successful in the future.
Do not take rejections personally. Instead, treat them as a part of the job and move on. Remember, real estate is a numbers game. The more prospects you reach out to, the more likely you are to find those who are a good fit for your services.

Finally, remember to stay positive. Maintaining a positive attitude, even in the face of objections and rejections, can make a big difference. It can help you stay motivated and focused, and it can also have a positive impact on your interactions with clients. After all, people prefer to work with agents who are optimistic and enthusiastic.

Remember, every objection and rejection is an opportunity to learn, grow, and improve. By adopting a strategic approach to handling these situations, you can become a more effective and successful real estate agent. So, keep these strategies in mind, and you'll be well on your way to becoming a world-class real estate agent.

How do you handle price negotiations?

Being a world-class real estate agent involves more than just showing properties and closing deals. It also involves the complex and delicate art of price negotiation. This skill is crucial for ensuring that your clients get the best possible deal, and it can make or break your reputation as an agent.

Let's explore some strategies and tactics that can help you handle price negotiations like a pro.

Understanding the Market

The first step in mastering negotiations is to understand the market inside and out. This knowledge provides you with a solid foundation to argue your client's case. Research recent sales in the area, understand the current demand and supply, and be aware of the economic factors that could influence the real estate market. This information will arm you with the facts you need to negotiate effectively.

Setting the Right Expectations

Whether you're representing the buyer or the seller, it's crucial to set the right expectations from the start. Explain to your clients that the listing price is just a starting point for negotiations. Encourage your selling clients to be flexible and realistic about their pricing, while advising your buying clients to be prepared to pay a fair price based on market conditions.

Building a Rapport

A positive relationship with the other party can significantly ease the negotiation process. Build a rapport and establish trust by being professional, respectful, and empathetic. Understand their needs, listen to their concerns, and show them that you're genuinely interested in reaching a solution that benefits everyone.

Developing a Negotiation Strategy

Every negotiation should have a strategy. Start by determining what your client's bottom line is. What's the minimum price your seller is willing to accept? What's the maximum price your buyer is willing to pay? Once you know these figures, you can formulate a strategy. For instance, if you're representing a buyer in a buyer's market, you might start by offering less than the asking price. However, if you're representing a seller in a seller's market, you might aim for a higher than asking price.

Staying Calm and Patient

Negotiations can be stressful, but it's important to stay calm and patient. Don't be pressured into making quick decisions. Take your time to review offers and counteroffers and discuss these with your clients. Make sure that every decision made is well thought out and in the best interest of your clients.

Communicating Clearly

Clear, concise, and confident communication is key in negotiations. Make sure that all terms and conditions are clearly communicated and understood by both parties. Remember, the goal is not just to close the deal, but to ensure that all parties are satisfied with the outcome.

Being Prepared to Walk Away

Sometimes, despite your best efforts, a satisfactory agreement can't be reached. In such cases, it might be in your client's best interest to walk away from the deal. It's better to wait for a deal that meets your client's needs than to settle for a less than optimal outcome.

Price negotiation is a critical skill for any real estate agent. It requires a deep understanding of the market, a well-thought-out strategy, and excellent communication skills. But most importantly, it requires the ability to put your client's needs first. By mastering this skill, you can ensure that your clients get the best possible deal and boost your reputation as a top-notch real estate agent.

How do you use technology and social media in real estate marketing?

In this digital age, technology and social media play a crucial role in any business, including real estate. As an aspiring world-class real estate agent, you must leverage these tools to reach a larger audience, engage potential clients, and boost sales. This question will guide you on how to effectively utilize technology and social media in your real estate marketing strategies.

Property Listings and Virtual Tours

The first step in using technology in real estate marketing is to create an online presence for your properties. Websites such as Zillow, Realtor.com, and Trulia allow you to list properties, complete with high-quality photographs and detailed descriptions.

But why stop at photos? With advancements in technology, you can now provide virtual tours of your properties. Using 360-degree cameras and virtual reality technology, you can create immersive tours that allow potential buyers to explore properties from the comfort of their own homes. This not only saves time but also broadens your reach to those who are unable to physically visit the properties.

Social Media Marketing

Social media platforms are powerful tools for reaching out to potential buyers. You can use platforms like Facebook, Instagram, and LinkedIn to promote your listings, share engaging content, and connect with your audience.

Facebook is an excellent platform for targeted advertising. You can use its Ad Manager tool to create advertisements for your listings, targeting specific demographics based on age, location, income, and more.

Instagram, with its visually driven platform, is perfect for showcasing high-quality images and videos of your properties. You can also use Instagram Stories for virtual property tours, behind-the-scenes looks, and to share customer testimonials.

LinkedIn allows you to connect with other real estate professionals and potential clients. By sharing industry-related articles and insights, you can establish yourself as a knowledgeable and trustworthy professional in the field.

Email Marketing

Email marketing remains one of the most effective ways to reach potential clients. Use technology to automate your email campaigns, sending out regular newsletters with market updates, new listings, and helpful tips for buyers and sellers. Remember to personalize your emails as much as possible to make your recipients feel valued and connected.

Customer Relationship Management (CRM) Systems

CRM systems are software tools that help manage client relationships and streamline processes. They can track interactions with potential and current clients, schedule appointments, and follow-up tasks, and even analyze data to identify trends and opportunities. Leveraging a CRM system can help you stay organized, improve customer service, and ultimately, close more deals.

Mobile Apps

Many buyers and sellers are now using mobile apps to search for properties. You can leverage this trend by providing a mobile-friendly website or even creating your own app. An app could provide features like property search, map integration, virtual tours, and direct messaging for quick and easy client communication.

technology and social media are no longer optional extras in real estate marketing - they're essential tools. As a world-class real estate agent, you must be tech-savvy and social media literate. Embrace these tools, invest time in learning how to use them effectively, and you will see a significant impact on your marketing reach and success.

5 ETHICS AND INTEGRITY

How important are ethics and integrity in real estate?

In the high-stakes world of real estate, the importance of ethics and integrity cannot be overstated. A world-class real estate agent maintains an impeccable reputation, and this reputation is grounded in a strong ethical compass and unwavering integrity. These key qualities not only differentiate you from other agents and promote customer trust, but they also contribute to the overall health and sustainability of the real estate industry at large.

Ethics, in this context, refers to the moral principles guiding an agent's interactions with clients, peers, and other stakeholders in real estate transactions. It entails adhering to a professional code of conduct that prioritizes honesty, fairness, and respect. For example, real estate agents must always disclose material facts about a property to potential buyers, even if such information could potentially hamper the sale. Misrepresenting a property by hiding its flaws is not only unethical but can also lead to legal consequences. The same applies to overpricing a property just to increase commission earnings.

Integrity, on the other hand, involves being truthful and consistent in all your actions, words, decisions, methods, and outcomes. It means doing the right thing even when no one is watching. A real estate agent with integrity will not exploit a client's lack of knowledge for personal gain. Instead, they will provide accurate and helpful information, even if it means losing a potential sale.

The importance of ethics and integrity in real estate can be examined from several perspectives:

Building Trust

Trust is fundamental in any business relationship, and real estate is no exception. Clients need to trust that an agent is acting in their best interest. An agent's ethics and integrity directly influence the level of trust a client can place in them. By being honest, fair, and reliable, you not only earn your client's trust but also their loyalty. This trust often translates into repeat business and referrals, which are crucial for a real estate agent's success.

Enhancing Professional Reputation

Your reputation as a real estate agent is your most valuable asset. Agents known for their ethical conduct and integrity are more likely to attract clients and build successful careers. A tarnished reputation, on the other hand, can harm your career in the long run. Given the power of word-of-mouth and online reviews in the real estate industry, maintaining a good reputation is paramount.

Legal Compliance

The real estate industry is heavily regulated, and agents are expected to comply with laws and regulations. Unethical behaviors can lead to hefty fines, license revocation, and even imprisonment. Upholding ethical standards and demonstrating integrity can save you from these potential legal troubles.

Industry Sustainability

The real estate industry thrives on trust and credibility. A lack of ethics and integrity among agents could damage the industry's reputation and deter potential buyers and sellers. Therefore, maintaining high ethical standards is necessary for the industry's long-term growth and sustainability.

Being a world-class real estate agent involves more than just mastering market trends and negotiation skills. It requires a steadfast commitment to ethics and integrity. By upholding these values, you can cultivate trust, enhance your reputation, avoid legal troubles, and contribute to a healthy and sustainable real estate industry. Remember, your reputation is your brand and maintaining ethical conduct and integrity is the best way to protect and enhance it.

How do you handle ethical dilemmas in your profession?

One of the essential aspects of being a world-class real estate agent is maintaining a high ethical standard. As a real estate agent, you will often come across situations where ethical dilemmas may arise. It may be a conflict of interest, a question of disclosure, or a matter of acting in the best interest of your client. How you navigate these dilemmas can greatly impact your reputation and career trajectory. This question discusses how to handle ethical dilemmas in the real estate profession.

The first step to dealing with an ethical dilemma is recognizing that you are in one. This isn't always as straightforward as it might seem. For instance, you might be representing both the buyer and the seller in a transaction. This dual representation could lead to a conflict of interest, where your duty to one client may interfere with your duty to another. Recognizing this ethical dilemma is the first step in addressing it.

Moreover, it's important to understand and adhere to the ethical guidelines and laws set forth by real estate governing bodies. In the United States, the National Association of Realtors (NAR) has established a Code of Ethics and Standards of Practice. This code provides a framework for ethical behavior and decision-making. Familiarize yourself with these guidelines and use them as a reference point when faced with ethical dilemmas.

When faced with an ethical dilemma, it can be helpful to seek counsel. This could be a mentor, a broker, or a legal advisor. They can provide you with an outside perspective, helping you see the bigger picture and consider aspects you might have overlooked. Also, they can share their own experiences and advice on how they handled similar situations.

Transparency is also crucial in handling ethical dilemmas. If you find yourself in a potential conflict of interest, it is essential to disclose it to all parties involved. Let your clients know about the situation and how you plan to handle it. This openness builds trust and can prevent misunderstandings down the line.

At times, resolving an ethical dilemma may involve difficult decisions. You may have to prioritize your ethical obligations over potential commissions or business relationships. For example, if a seller doesn't want to disclose a property's defects to a potential buyer, you have a moral and legal obligation to do so. This may strain your relationship with the seller and even cost you a sale, but it is the ethical course of action.

Lastly, always strive to act in the best interest of your clients. This is a guiding principle in real estate and a cornerstone of ethical behavior. It means putting your clients' needs and interests before your own and providing them with the best service possible. It involves being honest, fair, and diligent in your dealings.

Dealing with ethical dilemmas is not always easy. It requires discernment, integrity, and sometimes sacrifice. But by handling these dilemmas professionally, you uphold the values of your profession and build a reputation as a trustworthy, world-class real estate agent. Remember, a successful real estate agent is not just measured by the number of sales they make, but by their conduct and the respect they earn from their clients and peers.

In the coming pages, we will discuss how to build lasting relationships with your clients – a key factor in a successful real estate career.

How does your agency maintain transparency with clients?

Transparency is an essential pillar in any successful real estate agency-client relationship. It is the benchmark of trust, professionalism, and ethical business practices. As a world-class real estate agent, it is pivotal to understand the importance of transparency and how to maintain it with all clients.

You need to uphold transparency in several ways. First, open and honest communication is essential at all stages of the property transaction process. Your clients should not be left in the dark regarding any aspect of their sale, purchase, or lease. You must share information about the market trends, pricing, contract details, and any legal issues that may affect the client's decision. Also, you should provide regular updates and maintain an open line of communication, so your clients feel involved and informed at each step.

Next, you need to uphold transparency through complete disclosure. This means you should provide all relevant information about a property, be it positive or negative, to the potential buyer or seller. It is your duty to reveal any known defects, structural issues, or legal encumbrances that may impact the value or enjoyment of the property. Ensure all disclosures are made in writing to avoid any misunderstandings or legal complications later on.

Thirdly, you need to maintain transparency by clearly stating your fees, commissions, and any other costs associated with the real estate transaction.

Ideally, you can provide a comprehensive breakdown of these costs to our clients before entering any agreement. This way, your clients can make informed decisions and understand exactly what they are paying for. No hidden fees, no surprise costs; just straightforward, honest business.

Moreover, you should strive to manage our clients' expectations realistically. The real estate market can be unpredictable, and it's natural for every client to desire the best outcome. However, creating illusions of a 'guaranteed sale' or promising unrealistic prices is not a best practice. Instead, use your expertise and knowledge to provide clients with realistic estimates and outcomes based on current market conditions.

You should respect your clients' privacy and confidentiality. Handle all personal and financial information with utmost discretion, ensuring it is securely stored and used solely for the purpose of the transaction. Ensure that we seek our clients' consent before sharing their information with any third parties.

Lastly, you should believe in the power of feedback. Encourage your clients to share their experiences, thoughts, and suggestions about your services. This open feedback system not only helps you improve and grow, but also allows potential clients to gauge our honesty, integrity, and effectiveness. With this feedback, you can strive to resolve any issues or concerns promptly and transparently, turning challenges into opportunities for improvement.

Maintaining transparency with clients is not just about ticking a box in the ethical code of conduct; it's about establishing a long-term relationship built on trust and mutual respect. It's about making clients feel valued, heard, and confident in their agent's ability to deliver. It's about standing by your word and delivering on your promises. This is the key to becoming a world-class real estate agent and making your mark in this competitive industry.

Remember, transparency is not merely a strategy; it's a philosophy that drives every decision, every interaction, and every transaction. Embrace it, and you're on your way to becoming the exceptional real estate agent you aspire to be.

How do you manage conflicts of interest?

In the realm of real estate, conflicts of interest can arise out of various situations. It could be representing both the buyer and the seller in a transaction, having personal relationships with clients, or having personal investment interests in properties. Understanding and managing these conflicts effectively is an imperative skill for a world-class real estate agent.

The first step in managing conflicts of interest is to acknowledge them. Ignorance or denial will not help in resolving these issues but will rather deteriorate the trust and relationship you have with your clients. It is also against the National Association of Realtors' code of ethics not to disclose conflicts of interest.

In situations where you are representing both the buyer and the seller, often referred to as dual agency, transparency is the key. It is crucial to disclose to both parties that you are representing the other as well. You should also explain the implications, such as the fact that you cannot share confidential information from one party with the other or advocate for one party against the other. If both parties are comfortable with the arrangement, it can proceed. Otherwise, it may be best to refer one party to another agent to avoid any potential conflict.

Personal relationships can also lead to conflicts of interest. If you have a close relationship with a client, it can cloud your judgment and compromise your ability to provide objective advice. In these cases, you should disclose the relationship to all parties involved and, if necessary, refer the client to another agent.

If you have a personal investment interest in a property, it can create a conflict of interest if you are also representing a buyer for that property. In this case, it is vital to disclose your interest to the buyer. Furthermore, you should avoid any actions that could be perceived as manipulating the price or the sale of the property to your advantage.

In all cases, it is essential to keep the best interests of your clients at the forefront. While it is not wrong to have personal interests or relationships, they should not affect your professional obligations. If you are unsure whether a situation presents a conflict of interest, consider seeking advice from an experienced colleague, your broker, or a real estate attorney.

Moreover, you should also establish a clear conflict of interest policy in your practice. This policy should set out the steps you will take to identify, disclose, and manage conflicts of interest. It can also provide guidance on when to decline representation or refer clients to another agent.

Lastly, always remember that trust is the cornerstone of any successful real estate practice. Clients need to trust that their agent is working in their best interest. This is why managing conflicts of interest is so important. By identifying and resolving these conflicts effectively, you can maintain your clients' trust and uphold your reputation as a world-class real estate agent. conflicts of interest are almost inevitable in the real estate industry. However, they do not need to negatively impact your relationships with your clients or your practice.

By being proactive, transparent, and putting your clients' interests first, you can manage these conflicts effectively and navigate the complex world of real estate with integrity and professionalism.

How do you ensure the confidentiality and privacy of your clients?

In the realm of real estate, trust is an essential component of every transaction. Your clients entrust you with personal and financial information that is vital to their real estate decisions. As a professional real estate agent, it is your responsibility to uphold the principles of confidentiality and privacy. This question outlines the key steps you can take to ensure the confidentiality and privacy of your clients.

Firstly, understanding the legal implications of privacy laws is crucial. Many countries have stringent laws regarding the use and disclosure of personal information. In the United States, for example, the Gramm-Leach-Bliley Act regulates the handling of personal information by financial institutions, which includes real estate agencies. Violation of these laws can lead to severe penalties, both financially and professionally. Therefore, familiarize yourself with the privacy legislation applicable in your area and follow it meticulously.

Next, create a clear privacy policy for your agency. This policy should detail how personal information is collected, used, stored, and destroyed. It should also specify the circumstances under which such information might be disclosed and to whom. Make sure to communicate this policy to your clients at the start of your relationship to ensure transparency. It's also wise to provide them with a written copy of the policy for their records.

Furthermore, treat every piece of information you receive from your clients as confidential unless they give explicit permission otherwise. This rule applies even if the information seems inconsequential. Remember, what may seem insignificant to you might be very important to your client. Always respect their wishes regarding the privacy of their information.

In today's digital age, data security is a paramount concern. Use secure systems to store client information. This might mean investing in high-quality software with built-in encryption to protect against data breaches. Regularly update your systems and use strong, unique passwords. Additionally, train your staff on proper data handling procedures and the importance of maintaining client confidentiality.

Avoid discussing clients and their transactions in public spaces where conversations can be overheard. If you must discuss sensitive information outside of the office, do so in a private setting, and keep the conversation as vague as possible.

Be cautious when disposing of documents that contain client information. Shredding is the most secure method of disposal and is recommended for any documents containing sensitive data. Digital files should be permanently deleted when no longer needed, and storage devices should be physically destroyed to prevent data recovery.

Lastly, if a data breach does occur, it's important to have a plan in place. This should include notifying the affected clients and any relevant regulatory bodies, working to mitigate the damage, and taking steps to prevent future breaches.

Keeping your clients' information confidential and secure is not only a legal obligation but also a professional one. By diligently following these guidelines, you can maintain your clients' trust, uphold your reputation as a reliable real estate agent, and ensure you are providing the highest level of service to your clients.

Remember, in the real estate profession, a client's trust is our most valuable asset. Without it, our ability to successfully serve our clients and grow our business is severely compromised. Therefore, it is of utmost importance that we make every effort to protect our clients' confidentiality and privacy. This commitment should be at the heart of everything we do as world-class real estate agents.

6 PROPERTY EVALUATION

How do you assess a property's condition?

The condition of a property is one of the most important factors that a real estate agent must assess. A keen understanding of a property's condition can help you as an agent to determine its value, negotiate its price, and market it effectively. This section will provide a comprehensive guide on how to assess a property's condition.

To begin, you must establish a systematic approach. Start with the exterior of the property and then move indoors. Document everything you observe; a detailed record will prove invaluable when making comparisons with other properties, determining the necessary renovations, and creating a compelling listing.

Exterior Inspection

The exterior condition of a property often creates the first impression for potential buyers. Start by examining the structural condition of the property. Look for signs of wear and tear, such as cracks in the walls, sagging roofs, or damaged gutters. These might indicate deeper structural problems that can significantly devalue the property.

Next, assess the condition of the paintwork, window frames, and doors. Peeling paint, rotten wood, and rusted metal are signs of neglect and might require costly repairs. Also, take note of the property's landscaping. A well-maintained garden can enhance a property's curb appeal and increase its market value.

Interior Inspection

When inspecting the interior, start with the structure. Look for signs of water damage, such as stains or mold on ceilings and walls. Inspect the floors for any unevenness or loose boards which could indicate structural issues. Check the condition of the windows and doors – they should open and close easily, and there should be no signs of broken seals in double glazed units.

Next, examine the condition of the utilities and fixtures. Check the electrical system, plumbing, heating, and cooling units. These are crucial for the livability of the property, and any issues could result in significant repair costs.
In the kitchen and bathroom, look at the condition of the fixtures and appliances. They should be functional and up-to-date. Outdated or broken appliances could detract from the property's value and might need to be replaced.

Finally, take a good look at the property's finishings, such as the paint, floor coverings, and light fixtures. These may seem minor, but they greatly influence a property's aesthetic appeal and can affect the overall valuation.

Professional Inspection
While a visual inspection can reveal a lot about a property's condition, some issues may not be immediately apparent. It is highly advisable to get a professional inspection. An experienced property inspector can identify hidden issues such as pest infestations, asbestos, faulty wiring, or plumbing issues. While this involves an additional cost, it can save you and your client from potential financial and legal complications down the line.

Assessing a property's condition is a critical skill for a real estate agent. It involves a detailed visual inspection of the property's exterior and interior, as well as a professional inspection to uncover any hidden issues. It's not just about identifying problems, but also about understanding their implications in terms of cost, value, and marketability. By doing this effectively, you can provide accurate advice to your clients, negotiate better deals, and enhance your reputation as a reliable and knowledgeable real estate agent.

How important are home inspections and appraisals in your profession?

The relevance of home inspections and appraisals in the real estate profession cannot be overstated. These two elements serve as the foundation upon which the credibility of transactions is built and are critical to succeed in the buy-sell process.

Home inspections and appraisals are not just boxes to tick off in a real estate deal. They are pivotal processes that can make or break a property transaction. They provide the most accurate picture of a property's condition and value, and offer an assurance of the investment to all parties involved. In this question, we will explore the importance of home inspections and appraisals, and how they contribute to the success of a real estate agent.

Home Inspections: The Eye for Detail

Home inspections are comprehensive evaluations of a property's structural and functional condition. A qualified home inspector assesses various aspects of a property, including its heating and cooling systems, plumbing, electrical work, water and sewage systems, doors and windows, roof, and foundation.

As a real estate agent, understanding the results of a home inspection is crucial for several reasons. Firstly, having a detailed home inspection report allows you to accurately represent the property's condition to potential buyers. This transparency not only builds trust but also protects you legally by preventing any future accusations of misrepresentation.

Secondly, a home inspection can be a powerful bargaining tool. If the inspection reveals significant issues, you can negotiate for a lower price or ask the seller to fix the problems before closing the deal. On the other hand, a clean inspection report can justify the asking price or even raise it in a competitive market. It's an opportunity for you to demonstrate your negotiation skills and commitment to your client's best interests.

Appraisals: The Value Proposition

While a home inspection is about the property's condition, an appraisal is about its value. A professional appraiser determines the property's market value based on its characteristics and comparables, i.e., the selling price of similar properties in the same area.

An accurate appraisal bears significant impact on a real estate transaction. For a buyer, it can provide an independent, unbiased view of the property's value, which is instrumental in securing a mortgage. Lenders typically won't provide a loan for more than the appraised value.

For a seller, a higher appraisal means they can justify a higher asking price.

As a real estate agent, it's your responsibility to ensure the appraisal process is unbiased and accurate, reflecting the true value of the property.

Both inspections and appraisals are crucial in guiding your clients through their real estate journey. They provide an objective view of the property's condition and value, helping your clients make informed decisions. By understanding these processes, you can better serve your clients, mitigate potential risks, and ensure a smooth transaction.

The importance of home inspections and appraisals in the real estate profession is immense. They are not just procedural necessities; they are instrumental in fostering trust, enabling informed decision-making, and ensuring fair and successful transactions. As a real estate agent aiming for world-class stature, mastering the knowledge and nuances of home inspections and appraisals is not an option; it's a necessity.

How do you determine the potential of a property for investment?

In real estate investment, the adage "location, location, location" is not the only crucial factor. Determining the potential of a property for investment involves a complex process of assessment that considers multiple factors. This question will guide you through the key aspects you need to consider to evaluate a property's investment potential.

Location
The location of a property determines its accessibility, desirability, and demand. Look at the proximity to amenities such as schools, hospitals, shopping centers, and public transportation. Consider the future development plans for the area. Remember, an area with planned infrastructure or commercial developments can enhance property values in the future. Also, consider the crime rate and overall safety of the neighborhood. All these factors affect the rental and resale value of the property.

Market Conditions:
In addition to the property's specific location, you also need to understand the wider real estate market conditions. Look at market trends, both current and forecasted. Are property prices rising or falling in the area? Is it a buyer's or a seller's market? What's the rental yield in the area? Analyzing

these conditions will give you an idea of the potential return on investment (ROI) and can help you decide whether it is the right time to invest.

Property Conditions
The physical condition of the property plays a significant role in determining its investment potential. Examine the property carefully for any structural issues, like foundation problems, roof leaks, plumbing issues, or electrical problems. Hiring a professional inspector can be a good idea to ensure you don't miss any potential issues. Major repairs can significantly affect your return on investment.

Financial Analysis
Financial analysis is critical in assessing the potential of a property for investment. Start by determining the total cost of the property, including purchase price, closing costs, and any immediate repairs or renovations needed. Compare this to the potential income from the property, either from rental income or from selling the property after improving it. This will help you calculate your potential ROI.

Also, consider the property's potential cash flow. If you're planning to rent the property, will the rental income cover your mortgage payment, property taxes, insurance, maintenance, and any property management costs? If not, you may find yourself subsidizing your investment each month.

Growth Potential
Look at the growth potential of the property. Is the area growing? Are new businesses moving in? Is there a strong job market? Areas with strong growth potential often lead to higher demand for housing, which can drive up property values and rental rates.

Exit Strategy
Finally, always have an exit strategy. If your investment doesn't go as planned, you need to have a clear plan of action to minimize your losses. This could include selling the property, converting it into a rental, or even living in it yourself.

Determining the potential of a property for investment is a multifaceted process that requires careful consideration and analysis. It's a critical skill for a world-class real estate agent, and mastering it will allow you to provide better advice to your clients and make more informed decisions in your own investments. Keep in mind that every property is unique, and what works for one property might not work for another. Therefore, each property must be evaluated individually, considering all the factors mentioned above.

How do you factor in the location and neighborhood in property evaluation?

One of the most crucial aspects of being a successful real estate agent is understanding the importance of location and neighborhood in property valuation. The idiom, 'location, location, location,' is often heard in the real estate industry, and for a good reason. It is the single most significant factor that determines a property's value – now and in the future. A property's location can make or break a sale, and it can significantly increase or decrease a property's overall value.

When factoring in location, several variables come into play. The proximity to amenities, the noise level, the neighborhood's safety, and access to public transportation or major highways are all key components to consider.

The first thing to evaluate is the proximity to amenities. Is the property close to schools, shops, restaurants, hospitals, and parks? These are essential conveniences that potential buyers look for. Having these facilities nearby not only adds to the property's appeal but also significantly boosts its value.

Noise level is another critical aspect. Although some may appreciate the hustle and bustle of city life, others may prefer a quieter, more peaceful environment. Properties in quiet, residential areas typically command higher prices than those in noisier, busier areas.

Safety is always a top concern for any homeowner. A neighborhood's safety profile can dramatically influence a property's value. Properties in safe, low-crime areas are likely to be more expensive than those in neighborhoods with higher crime rates. Utilize crime statistics and local police reports to get an accurate understanding of the neighborhood's safety.

Access to public transportation and major highways is another important factor. Properties that provide easy access to public transit and highways are generally more desirable, especially in urban settings where traffic can be an issue.

After considering the macro factors, it's time to evaluate the micro factors, which involve the immediate surroundings of the property. These include the condition of neighboring properties, the presence of vacant or run-down buildings, and the type of buildings in the vicinity.

The condition of neighboring properties can significantly affect a property's value. If neighboring properties are well-maintained, they can enhance the value of the property in question. On the other hand, dilapidated or vacant properties can devalue an otherwise appealing property.

Additionally, the type of buildings in the neighborhood can influence a property's value. For example, a residential property situated amidst commercial buildings may not fetch as high a price as one located in a purely residential area.

Lastly, consider future developments. If the neighborhood is set to benefit from future infrastructural developments, such as a new school or shopping center, these can potentially increase the property's value. However, adverse future developments, like a landfill or industrial park, can decrease the property's value.

It's important to remember that although some factors can negatively impact a property's value, they can also create opportunities for savvy investors looking for a bargain. For instance, properties in up-and-coming neighborhoods might have lower current values but hold the promise of significant future appreciation.

As a real estate agent, it's your responsibility to provide a comprehensive understanding of how location and neighborhood influence property value. By doing so, you help your clients make informed decisions, whether they're buying a family home or making an investment. Therefore, understanding the factors outlined in this question and applying them in your property evaluation is key to becoming a successful real estate agent.

How do you evaluate a commercial property?

Evaluating commercial property is a crucial aspect of being a world-class real estate agent. This process involves a comprehensive analysis of the property's financial, structural and market-related aspects. Whether you're working with an investor, a business owner, or a developer, your ability to appraise a commercial property accurately can make or break a deal.

Financial Analysis

The financial health of a commercial property is a significant determinant of its overall worth. The first step in this direction is to examine the property's income and expenses. The income includes not just the rent obtained from tenants but also any additional income from vending machines, parking, etc. Subtract the operating expenses from the total income to calculate the Net Operating Income (NOI). The NOI is a reliable indicator of how profitable the property is before considering taxes and mortgage payments. Further, you can use the NOI to calculate the capitalization rate or cap rate, which gives the potential return on the investment.

Also, consider the property's potential for appreciation. While predicting future value can be tricky, looking at the property's historical data and market trends can provide some insight.

Structural Evaluation

The physical condition of the property is another major factor to consider. Conduct a thorough walkthrough of the property, noting any visible defects or potential issues. Look at the age of the building, the state of the roof, the HVAC system, plumbing, electrical systems, and the overall maintenance level.

It's advisable to hire a professional inspector to identify latent defects and provide an estimate for necessary repairs. This process can prevent unexpected costs in the future.

Location Analysis

Location is a critical factor in commercial real estate. The property should be in an area that's convenient for customers, employees, and suppliers. Consider factors such as proximity to highways, public transportation, and parking facilities.

Furthermore, look at the neighborhood's growth prospects. Are businesses in the area thriving? Is there new development in the vicinity? Are there any planned infrastructure projects that could impact the property's value?

Market Evaluation

An understanding of the local market conditions can offer insights into the property's potential for profitability. Research the commercial rental rates in the area, the vacancy rates, and the demand for the type of property you're evaluating.

Consider macroeconomic factors as well, such as the health of the economy, interest rates, and trends in the commercial real estate market.

Legal Considerations

Ensure the property complies with all zoning and land-use regulations. Also, check for any potential environmental issues or liabilities. If the property is a leased one, carefully review the lease agreements. Look at the lease lengths, rental rates, and terms of lease escalation.

Evaluating a commercial property is a multifaceted process that involves a deep understanding of financial analysis, property inspection, market trends, and legal considerations. As a real estate agent, your role is to provide your clients with a comprehensive, accurate assessment that will guide their decision-making process. Remember, your evaluation could be the difference between a lucrative investment and a costly mistake, so approach this task with the diligence and thoroughness it deserves.

In the following sections, we will delve deeper into each of these aspects, providing you with practical tools and techniques to refine your evaluation skills.

7 REAL ESTATE TRANSACTIONS

How do you guide a client through a real estate transaction?

The primary role of a real estate agent is to guide clients through the complex and often overwhelming process of real estate transactions. This process requires a comprehensive understanding of the real estate market, excellent communication skills, and a genuine commitment to your client's best interests.

The first step in guiding a client through a real estate transaction is the consultation stage. Here, you need to understand your client's needs and goals. Ask them questions about their budget, the type of property they're interested in, their preferred locations, and their timeline. They may be first-time homebuyers, seasoned investors, or sellers looking to downsize. Each client's circumstances will be unique, and as an agent, you need to tailor your approach accordingly.

Once you understand your client's needs, the next step is to educate them about the process. For buyers, explain the steps involved in buying a property, including pre-approval for a mortgage, property inspections, negotiations, and closing. For sellers, explain the process of listing their property, marketing strategies, negotiating offers, and closing the sale. Many clients will be unfamiliar with real estate jargon, so be sure to explain concepts in simple, easy-to-understand terms.

Finding the right property is a critical part of the transaction. Use your knowledge of the local market to identify properties that match your client's criteria. When showing properties, be honest about the pros and cons. Your client needs to trust that you are acting in their best interest, not just trying to make a sale.

Once your client has chosen a property, your role as a guide becomes even more crucial. Buyers need to be guided through the process of making an offer, negotiating terms, and understanding a purchase agreement. As the agent, you will be the primary communicator between your client and the seller's agent. You need to be a strong negotiator, ensuring your client gets the best possible deal.

For sellers, you need to guide them through receiving and evaluating offers. Help them understand the terms of each offer and advise them on the best course of action. This may involve negotiating for a higher price or better terms.

The closing process can be particularly stressful for clients. As their agent, you need to guide them through the final steps. This includes the home inspection, appraisal, final walk-through, and the actual closing where the title is transferred. You should be proactive in solving any issues that arise, always keeping your client's needs in mind.

Throughout the entire transaction process, communication is key. Keep your client updated at every stage. This not only reassures them that progress is being made, but it also helps to build trust. They need to know that you are working diligently on their behalf and that you are available to answer any questions they may have.

Finally, remember that your role as a guide does not end once the transaction is complete. Offer to help your client with post-transaction tasks, such as moving and setting up utilities. This extra level of service will be appreciated by your clients and can lead to repeat business and referrals.

Guiding a client through a real estate transaction requires a combination of market knowledge, communication skills, negotiation skills, and a deep commitment to serving your client's best interests. By mastering these, you can provide a smooth and successful transaction experience for your clients and establish yourself as a world-class real estate agent.

How do you explain the contractual terms and conditions to a client?

One of the most critical responsibilities of a real estate agent is effectively explaining contractual terms and conditions to clients. This is a complex task that requires a deep understanding of the legal language, an ability to communicate clearly and effectively, and a dedication to client service and understanding. This question will guide you on how to navigate this process.

The first step in explaining contractual terms to a client is ensuring that you understand them yourself. Real estate contracts are legal documents filled with terminology that can be hard to comprehend for those not familiar with the law. Therefore, it's crucial to familiarize yourself with the standard terms and conditions contained in most real estate contracts and understand their implications. It would be best if you also stayed up-to-date with any changes in real estate laws and regulations that could affect these contracts.

After gaining a comprehensive understanding of the terms, the next step is to break down this information in a way that your clients can understand. Avoid using technical jargon without explanation. Instead, use simple, everyday language to explain the terms of the contract. Keep in mind that your job is not to intimidate your clients with legal jargon but to enlighten them and help them make the best possible decisions.

A helpful strategy is to use analogies or metaphors to explain complex terms. For instance, you could compare the property buying process to a journey, with the contract serving as a roadmap, guiding the client to their destination: owning the property. This can help the client visualize the process and better understand the contract's role.

The explanation should cover all the critical areas of the contract, including the property's description, the purchase price, the down payment, the closing date, contingencies, and disclosures. It is also crucial to explain the obligations of both the buyer and the seller, the consequences of breaching the contract, and the steps that would be followed if a dispute arises.

While explaining, it's important to encourage your clients to ask questions. A common mistake that real estate agents make is assuming that the client understands everything. Always ask your clients if they have any questions or if they need further clarification on a point. This can help make sure they fully understand the contract and can make informed decisions.

In addition, it's beneficial to provide your clients with written materials that summarize the key points of the contract. These materials can serve as a reference for clients as they review the contract and make decisions.

Finally, and perhaps most importantly, remember to advise your clients that they should consult with a lawyer before signing any contract. As a real estate agent, you can explain the general terms and conditions of a contract, but you are not qualified to provide legal advice. Therefore, it's always a good idea for clients to have a lawyer review the contract.

explaining contractual terms and conditions to clients is a crucial part of a real estate agent's job. It requires a deep understanding of real estate contracts, an ability to communicate clearly and effectively, and a dedication to ensuring that clients understand what they are signing. By following these steps, you can help your clients navigate the complex world of real estate contracts and make informed decisions that serve their best interests.

How do you facilitate the negotiation process between buyers and sellers?

Negotiation in real estate is a critical skill and is often the deciding factor in closing a successful deal. As a real estate agent, you are the intermediary between the buyer and the seller, and your role is to facilitate the negotiation process, ensuring both parties reach a mutually satisfying agreement.

The negotiation process begins with a thorough understanding of both buyer's and seller's needs. As an agent, it's crucial to gather as much information as possible about both parties. This involves understanding the seller's motivations for selling, their preferred timeline, and the lowest price they are willing to accept. Similarly, for buyers, understand their budget, criteria for the ideal property, and their timeline for moving. The more information you have, the more effectively you can mediate between the two parties.

Effective communication is the cornerstone of successful negotiation. Throughout the negotiation process, you must keep both parties informed about each other's positions without revealing confidential information. This delicate balance requires tact and diplomacy. Be upfront and honest with both parties but remember your fiduciary duty to your client.

Strategizing is another essential aspect of the negotiation process. You need to devise a plan based on the information you have gathered. For instance, if a seller is in a rush to sell, they may be willing to negotiate more on the price. On the other hand, if a buyer has been searching for a long time and the property meets their specific requirements, they may be willing to pay a premium. Being aware of these dynamics can help you strategize effectively and guide your client towards making the right offer or counteroffer.

During the negotiation, it's crucial to maintain a calm and professional demeanor. Emotions can run high, but as the facilitator, you must stay neutral and focused on the end goal: a successful property transaction. Encourage both parties to look at the big picture rather than getting caught up in minor details. Remind them of their primary objectives and how the transaction serves those objectives.

Patience is a virtue in real estate negotiation. While some deals may close quickly, others may require a significant amount of time. It's essential not to rush the process. Allow both parties to take the time they need to consider offers, and don't pressure them into making quick decisions. This patience will build trust and increase the likelihood of a successful outcome.

Finally, remember that negotiation is not a zero-sum game. The goal is not for one party to 'win' at the expense of the other, but to find a solution that satisfies both parties. This perspective will help you facilitate negotiations in a way that creates a win-win situation, where both the buyer and the seller feel they have achieved their objectives.

Facilitating the negotiation process between buyers and sellers involves a deep understanding of both parties' needs, effective communication, strategic planning, and patience. By mastering these skills, you can act as an effective intermediary and help your clients navigate the complex process of buying or selling property. Your goal as a real estate agent is to ensure that both parties walk away from the transaction feeling satisfied and well-served.

How do you handle transaction disputes?

As a real estate agent, you are bound to encounter transaction disputes at some point in your career. These squabbles could arise over a variety of issues - from commission splits to contract stipulations, or even hidden defects discovered after the sale. It is essential that you equip yourself with the knowledge and skills to handle these disputes professionally and effectively to maintain your reputation and client relationships.

The first step to managing transaction disputes is understanding your role. As a real estate agent, your responsibility is to represent your client's interests. However, you also have a duty to act in a fair and honest manner with all parties, as dictated by the National Association of Realtors' Code of Ethics. Striking a balance between these two duties lies at the heart of dispute resolution.

Effective communication is one of the most critical skills in resolving transaction disputes. Miscommunication or lack of transparency often fuels disputes. To avoid this, ensure that you clearly communicate all terms, conditions, and expectations from the onset of the transaction. Keep all parties updated about any changes or developments. Moreover, consider using written communication whenever possible, as it provides a clear record of what was discussed and agreed upon.

However, despite your best efforts, disputes may still arise. When they do, remember to remain calm and professional. Avoid getting defensive or taking the dispute personally. Instead, focus on gathering as much information about the dispute as possible. Ask probing questions and listen actively to all parties involved. This will help you understand the root cause of the dispute and identify potential solutions.

Once you have a firm grasp of the problem, assess your options. Depending on the nature of the dispute, you might need to consult with your broker or a real estate attorney. They can provide you with legal advice and help you navigate any complex legal issues. Additionally, if the dispute is regarding the contract terms, you may need to refer back to the contract itself. It's crucial to have a thorough understanding of the contract and any implications it may have on the dispute.

After gathering all necessary information and advice, start working on resolving the dispute. Present the facts objectively and propose a fair resolution. Be prepared to negotiate and compromise. Remember, the goal is not to 'win' the dispute but to reach a solution that is acceptable to all parties.

In some cases, a dispute may not be resolvable through negotiation alone. You may need to involve a mediator or arbitrator to facilitate a resolution. Mediation is a voluntary process where a neutral third party helps the disputing parties reach a mutually acceptable solution. Arbitration, on the other hand, involves a third party who listens to both sides and makes a binding decision.

The key to successfully handling transaction disputes is to approach them with patience, professionalism, and a commitment to resolving them fairly. Do not shy away from seeking legal advice when necessary and always aim for a resolution that maintains the relationships you've worked hard to build.

Finally, remember that every dispute offers a learning opportunity. Reflect on what caused the dispute and how it was handled. Identify any areas for improvement and use this knowledge to prevent similar issues in the future. By doing so, you will not only become a better real estate agent but also a more effective problem solver, greatly enhancing your professional reputation.

How do you ensure a smooth closing process?

The closing process is the final hurdle in the real estate transaction, where the buyer finally becomes the owner of the property. It involves numerous steps and parties; thus, it can be overwhelming. However, as a real estate agent, your role is critical in ensuring a smooth closing process. Here's how you can make the process seamless and trouble-free.

Clear Communication
The first and foremost key to a smooth closing is clear and consistent communication. This is not just restricted to communicating with the buyer or seller. It involves keeping all parties, including mortgage brokers, appraisers, inspectors, and lawyers, in the loop. Regular updates about the progress of the transaction can help avoid misunderstandings and conflicts that can delay the closing process.

Organization
As a real estate agent, your organizational skills will be put to the test during the closing process. There will be numerous documents to manage, ranging from the purchase agreement to inspection reports, title deeds, and loan papers. Ensure that you have all these documents organized and readily accessible. Verify that all necessary signatures and initials are in place and that copies are distributed to all relevant parties.

Preparing the Clients
The closing process can be complex and daunting for many buyers and sellers, particularly those who are first-time participants in a real estate

transaction. Explain the closing process to your clients in detail, and let them know what to expect. Ensure they are aware of the costs involved, such as closing costs and down payments, and that they are prepared to meet these financial obligations.

Inspection and Appraisal

Ensuring the property passes its inspection and appraisal is another crucial step. The inspection is a potential deal-breaker; thus, it's essential to prepare the sellers for it and encourage them to make any necessary repairs. The property appraisal should reflect the agreed-upon purchase price. If it comes in low, you may need to renegotiate the price, which could delay the closing.

Contingency Clauses

Make sure that all contingency clauses in the contract, such as those relating to financing or the property passing inspection, have been met. If these contingencies aren't satisfied, the buyer has the right to back out of the deal without losing their earnest money deposit.

Final Walkthrough

Arrange for a final walkthrough of the property before the closing. This gives the buyers an opportunity to ensure that the property is in the condition they expect, and that any agreed-upon repairs have been completed.

Closing Agent

A closing agent, who might be a representative from a title company or a lawyer, will guide you and your clients through the final steps of the transaction. Make sure to coordinate with the closing agent to ensure they have all the necessary documents and information for the closing day.

Day of Closing

On the day of closing, reassure your clients and help them understand the documents they will be signing. Ensure they have the necessary funds for the closing costs and down payments. After all the paperwork is signed and the payment is completed, the keys can be handed over to the buyer.

By adhering to these steps, you can ensure a smooth closing process. Remember, your role as a real estate agent is to facilitate and guide your clients through this complex process. Your expertise, patience, and diligence can make the difference between a stressful ordeal and a successful, satisfying experience that culminates in the sale or purchase of a property.

8 PROPERTY MANAGEMENT

What are the responsibilities of a property manager?

In the real estate industry, property managers play an integral role in maintaining the value and generating income from properties. They are the bridge between property owners and tenants, providing an essential service to both parties. Let's explore the multifaceted responsibilities of a property manager.

Tenant Management
One of the primary responsibilities of a property manager is managing tenants. This process includes finding and screening potential tenants, handling leases, managing complaints, and initiating evictions when necessary. A good property manager ensures that the tenants are satisfied and that their concerns are addressed promptly. They will also understand and comply with housing laws and regulations, ensuring all interactions and transactions with tenants are legal and fair.

Rent Responsibilities
Property managers are responsible for setting, collecting, adjusting, and even enforcing rent. The initial rent level is decided based on market research to ensure that it's competitive while also generating revenue for the owner. Rent collection procedures are clearly outlined, ensuring timely payment from tenants. Adjustments and increases, aligned with municipal or state laws, are also managed by the property manager.

Maintenance and Repairs
The upkeep of the property is a major part of a property manager's job. This responsibility includes regular maintenance, emergency repairs, and renovations. They need to keep the property in safe and habitable condition, responding to tenant's repair requests promptly and handling

preventive property maintenance to keep everything in good working order. Hiring, managing, and coordinating with other workers like contractors, tradespeople, or maintenance workers also falls under their responsibilities.

Knowledge of Landlord-Tenant Laws

A good property manager must have a solid understanding of national and statewide landlord-tenant laws concerning tenant screening, safety and property conditions, eviction processes, lease addendums, terminating leases, handling security deposits, and rent collection. Understanding these laws helps them to avoid potential legal issues and lawsuits.

Budget and Records Management

Property managers are typically responsible for managing the budget of the property, keeping thorough records. This includes operational expenses, maintenance costs, rent collection, insurance, taxes, and more. All these financial transactions and interactions with tenants, suppliers, and maintenance services must be documented and organized for transparency, reporting, and future reference.

Marketing and Occupancy

A vacant property is a cost to the owner, so it's the property manager's job to ensure that the properties under their care are occupied. This involves understanding the market and potential target audience, effectively promoting the property, and even working on improving the property's aesthetics or functionality to increase its appeal.

Overall Property Management Strategy

Property managers often advise property owners on the potential profitability of their properties. They can provide valuable input on the benefits and drawbacks of different policies, as well as the financial implications of each decision. They can help develop a comprehensive management strategy that aims to maximize the owner's profit while minimizing their expenses.

A property manager serves as the custodian of the property, ensuring that it's managed efficiently and profitably, while maintaining a pleasant living environment for tenants. They carry out a broad spectrum of tasks from administrative to hands-on maintenance work, making them an indispensable part of the real estate industry. Their role requires a blend of people skills, knowledge of the property market, understanding of laws and regulations, and organizational capabilities. Whether for a single property or a large real estate portfolio, their contribution to maintaining and enhancing the value of the property is immense.

How do you handle property maintenance issues?

In the realm of property management, effective handling of property maintenance issues is not only necessary, but it's a crucial aspect that can make or break your reputation as a real estate agent. Whether you are managing residential or commercial properties, your ability to address such issues promptly and efficiently will set you apart as a world-class agent. In this question, we will explore key steps to handle property maintenance issues.

Firstly, it's important to have a clear understanding of what property maintenance entails. This includes the upkeep of a property, ensuring it remains in a safe, livable, and operable condition. Maintenance issues can range from minor problems like leaky faucets or broken light bulbs to major issues such as electrical faults or structural damages. These issues need proper attention to ensure the property remains attractive and habitable.

Regular Property Inspections
Conducting regular property inspections is a proactive approach to property maintenance. This allows you to identify any potential issues before they escalate into larger, more costly problems. Make it a point to inspect the property every few months. Check the roofing, plumbing, electrical systems, HVAC units, and structural integrity. Make sure to document these inspections for future reference.

Maintaining Good Relationships with Contractors
As a real estate agent, you need to have a reliable network of professionals such as plumbers, electricians, and carpenters who you can call upon when required. Cultivate good relationships with these contractors. This will ensure that you have someone to turn to who will promptly and effectively handle any maintenance issues that may arise.

Communication is Key
Keep an open line of communication with your tenants. Encourage them to report any maintenance issues they encounter promptly. Assure them that their comfort and safety are your top priorities. This will not only help in early detection of problems but also foster good relationships with tenants, which is crucial for the real estate business.

Efficient Management System

Consider using a property management software system that can help you keep track of all maintenance requests, as well as the status of any ongoing repairs. Such systems can also help in scheduling regular inspections, sending reminders, and documenting all maintenance activities.

Budget for Maintenance

A smart real estate agent knows that property maintenance is not an area where you can afford to cut corners. Always allocate a portion of your budget for routine maintenance and emergency repairs. This will ensure that you are financially prepared to handle any issues that may arise, thereby maintaining the value and attractiveness of the property.

Dealing with Emergency Situations

In cases of emergencies such as a fire outbreak, major leaks, or power outages, it's crucial to have a well-defined emergency response plan in place. This plan should detail steps to contain and manage the situation, ensuring the safety of all occupants.

Handling property maintenance issues as a real estate agent involves a mixture of proactive measures, efficient management, and prompt response to issues. By adopting these practices, you can ensure that properties under your management are well-maintained, safe, and attractive to potential clients. Remember, your ability to handle property maintenance issues effectively can significantly contribute to your reputation and success as a world-class real estate agent.

How do you ensure the property is ready for showing?

The art of selling a property extends far beyond your negotiation skills and market understanding. One of the most crucial aspects of being a successful real estate agent is the ability to present the property in the best possible light. The first impression is often the lasting one, so it is critical that the property is ready for showing. Here are some key steps to ensure that.

Deep Cleaning

The first step is to ensure the property is cleaned thoroughly. A spotless house not only looks inviting, but it also signals to potential buyers that the property has been well-maintained. All surfaces should be dust-free, carpets and floors should be cleaned, and windows should be clear and streak-free. Bathrooms and kitchens need special attention as they can be deal-breakers if not clean. If the property is large or particularly dirty, consider hiring a professional cleaning service.

De-Clutter

A cluttered home can seem smaller and less appealing. Ensure the property is de-cluttered, with enough open space to allow potential buyers to visualize their own belongings in the place. This might involve removing some furniture or personal items. Remember, you're trying to sell the house, not the items in it.

Repair and Maintenance

Attend to all the small repair tasks that have been pending for a while. This could be anything from a leaking faucet to a squeaky door. While these minor issues might not seem like a big deal, they can create an impression of a poorly maintained property.

Neutralize

Potential buyers should be able to imagine themselves living in the house. This can be difficult if the home is heavily personalized. Consider neutralizing the decor, using neutral hues for walls, and removing any personal or polarizing items.

Staging

Staging a property can significantly increase its appeal. This involves arranging furniture and decor to highlight the property's strengths and downplay its weaknesses. The idea is to make the home as appealing as possible to potential buyers. If you're not confident in your staging abilities, consider hiring a professional.

Lighting

Good lighting can make a property look warm, inviting, and spacious. Ensure all the bulbs are working and use the right type of lighting for each room. Open the curtains and blinds to let in as much natural light as possible.

Outdoor Spaces

Don't overlook the outdoor areas. A well-maintained yard, clean walkways, and a welcoming entrance can significantly enhance the curb appeal of the property.

Inviting Smells

Smell has a powerful impact on perception, so ensure the property smells fresh and inviting. Avoid strong scents, as they can be polarizing, and stick to universally appealing smells like freshly baked cookies or clean laundry.

Final Walkthrough
Just before the showing, do a final walkthrough of the property to ensure everything is in place. Check for cleanliness, lighting, temperature, and open all the doors and windows to let in fresh air.

Remember, when potential buyers walk into a property, they're not just looking at a house; they're looking for a potential home. Every detail matters, and as a real estate agent, it's up to you to present the property in a way that allows them to envision a happy and comfortable life there. Taking the time to prepare a property for showing will not only increase its appeal but also its perceived value, helping you close deals more quickly and at better prices.

How do you manage tenant relationships?

As a real estate agent, you will encounter a wide array of personalities and situations in your daily interactions with tenants. Your ability to manage tenant relationships will significantly influence your success within this industry. A harmonious landlord-tenant relationship not only fosters a positive environment but also ensures the smooth running of your business. Here are some strategies you can employ to effectively manage tenant relationships.

Clear Communication
The cornerstone of any successful relationship is clear, respectful, and consistent communication. Ensure that all communication, whether oral or written, is professional and courteous. Keep your tenants informed about important issues such as repairs, inspections, rent increases, or changes in property management. When tenants raise concerns or complaints, listen attentively and respond promptly.

Understand and Respect Tenant Rights
Familiarize yourself with the local and national laws governing tenant rights. As a real estate agent, you must respect these rights and avoid any actions that infringe upon them. Tenants have a right to privacy, safe and habitable living conditions, and freedom from discrimination. Violating these rights

can lead to legal consequences and damage your reputation.

Prompt Response to Maintenance and Repair Requests

As a real estate agent, you are responsible for ensuring that the properties you manage are in good condition. Prompt response to repair and maintenance requests is not only a legal obligation but also a way of showing respect for your tenants. It communicates that you value them and are committed to providing them with a comfortable living environment.

Treat Tenants with Respect and Fairness

Treat all tenants fairly and without discrimination. Avoid favoritism or bias, as this can lead to resentment and conflicts. Respect their privacy by providing adequate notice before entering their units, unless it's an emergency.

Conflict Resolution

Disputes between tenants and landlords are inevitable. How you handle these conflicts can make or break your relationship with your tenants. When dealing with conflicts, remain calm and professional. Listen to both sides of the story, and try to find a mutually agreeable solution. If necessary, enlist the help of a mediator or legal professional.

Regular Property Inspections

Regular inspections not only help you maintain the value of your property but also show your tenants that you are invested in providing them with a quality living environment. However, remember to provide your tenants with adequate notice before conducting inspections to avoid infringing on their privacy.

Provide Clear Lease Agreements

A clear and comprehensive lease agreement is a key tool in managing tenant relationships. It sets out the rights and responsibilities of both parties, reducing the potential for misunderstandings and disputes. Ensure your tenants understand the terms of the lease before they sign it.

Practice Empathy

Lastly, remember to practice empathy. Moving can be a stressful time, and tenants will appreciate a property manager who is understanding and accommodating. This could mean being flexible with moving dates, or understanding when a tenant has to break a lease due to unforeseen circumstances.

Managing tenant relationships is a delicate balancing act that requires excellent communication skills, a solid understanding of tenant rights, and a genuine respect for the people who live in your properties. By adopting these strategies, you can build strong relationships with your tenants, leading to a more stable and successful real estate business.

How do you handle lease agreements and evictions?

As a real estate agent, you will often find yourself in situations where you need to manage lease agreements and even handle evictions. This is an integral part of your job, and doing it well requires a thorough understanding of the law, as well as excellent interpersonal skills.

Lease Agreements
A lease agreement is a legally binding contract between a landlord and a tenant. It outlines the terms and conditions of the lease, including the duration of the lease, the amount of rent to be paid, the responsibilities of both parties, and the penalties for breach of contract.

As a real estate agent, your role is to ensure that the lease agreement is fair and reasonable to both parties. This means carefully reviewing the terms of the agreement, negotiating any changes that may be necessary, and ensuring that both parties understand their rights and responsibilities under the agreement.

To do this effectively, you need to have a solid understanding of local rental laws and market conditions. You should also be able to explain legal jargon in layman's terms so that both landlords and tenants fully understand the agreement they're entering into.

It's important to remember that a lease agreement is not just a business transaction; it's also a relationship. As such, it's crucial to foster a positive relationship between landlords and tenants. This can be achieved by ensuring that the lease agreement is fair, transparent, and respects the rights and interests of both parties.

Evictions
Unfortunately, there will be times when it becomes necessary to evict a tenant. This could be due to a variety of reasons, including non-payment of rent, breach of the lease agreement, or property damage.

Evictions are often stressful and emotionally charged situations, and handling them requires sensitivity, tact, and a firm understanding of the law.

First and foremost, it's important to understand that evictions must be carried out in accordance with the law. This means following the proper legal procedures, which typically involve giving the tenant a notice of eviction, allowing them a certain period of time to rectify the situation, and obtaining a court order if necessary.

As a real estate agent, your role in this process is to guide and support your client, the landlord, through the legal process. This includes explaining the eviction process, helping to draft the eviction notice, and representing the landlord in court if necessary.

However, it's also important to remember that eviction should be a last resort. In many cases, conflicts between landlords and tenants can be resolved through communication and negotiation. As a real estate agent, your communication and negotiation skills can be invaluable in these situations. You can often help to mediate between the parties, find a mutually acceptable solution, and prevent the situation from escalating to eviction.

Handling lease agreements and evictions is a challenging but essential part of your role as a real estate agent. It requires a deep understanding of the law, excellent communication and negotiation skills, and a commitment to fairness and respect for all parties.

9 FINANCING REAL ESTATE TRANSACTIONS

What are the different types of real estate financing?

As a real estate agent, understanding the different types of real estate financing is crucial. This knowledge is a fundamental tool that will enable you to better serve your clients and help them find the best financing method for their needs. There are several financing options available, each with its own advantages, disadvantages, and unique requirements. This question aims to provide a comprehensive overview of the various types of real estate financing.

Conventional Loans
This type of loan is the most common form of real estate financing. Offered by private lenders like banks, credit unions, and mortgage companies, conventional loans are not backed by any government entity. Borrowers will typically need a good credit score, a stable income, and a reasonable debt-to-income ratio to qualify. Conventional loans require a down payment, which can range from 3% to 20% or more of the property's purchase price.

Federal Housing Administration (FHA) Loans
These loans are insured by the federal government and are designed to help lower income and first-time homebuyers. They require a smaller down payment (as low as 3.5%) and are more forgiving with credit scores. However, borrowers must pay for mortgage insurance, which increases the overall cost of the loan.

Veterans Administration (VA) Loans
VA loans are available to active duty military members, veterans, and certain surviving spouses. These loans require no down payment and do not require mortgage insurance. However, they do have a one-time funding

fee that can be rolled into the loan amount.

USDA Loans

Offered by the United States Department of Agriculture, these loans are designed for rural property buyers who meet specific income requirements. They offer 100% financing, meaning no down payment is required, and include low interest rates.

Bridge Loans

A bridge loan is a short-term loan that helps buyers bridge the gap between the cost of a new home and the sale of the current home. This loan can be useful when a buyer needs to move quickly and doesn't have time to sell their existing home.

Home Equity Loans

Home equity loans are a type of second mortgage where the lender gives the borrower a lump sum that they repay over a set term, usually 5 to 15 years. The loan amount is based on the value of the homeowner's equity.

Hard Money Loans

These are typically short-term, high-interest loans provided by private investors or companies. They are often used for investment properties or when the borrower cannot qualify for a conventional mortgage.

Interest-Only Loans

With interest-only loans, borrowers pay only the interest on the loan for a certain period. This can make the initial payments more affordable, but the principal balance does not decrease during the interest-only period.

Each of these financing options serves different purposes and has its own set of qualifications. As a real estate agent, your role is to guide your clients through these options and help them choose the one that best suits their financial situation and property goals. Remember, the most appropriate financing method will depend on a variety of factors, including the client's credit score, income, down payment ability, and personal preferences.

Next, we will delve deeper into each of these financing types, providing you with a more in-depth understanding of their requirements, benefits, and drawbacks. This knowledge will equip you to guide your clients confidently and professionally through their real estate financing journey.

How do you advise clients on financing options?

Navigating the Labyrinth of Financing: Guiding Clients Towards the Best Option

In the dynamic world of real estate, the role of an agent extends beyond finding the right property or selling one; it is about facilitating the entire process to ensure a seamless experience for the client. Among these responsibilities, one of the most critical is advising clients on financing options. With a plethora of mortgage products and finance routes available in the market, making an informed decision can be an overwhelming task for clients.

The first step in advising clients on financing options is to understand their financial situation, needs, and long-term goals. This understanding is key to outlining the best possible financial strategies. An agent needs to have a candid discussion with the clients about their savings, credit score, income stability, existing debts, and future financial plans. It is also essential to understand the purpose of the purchase - whether it is for personal use, investment, or flipping.

With a thorough understanding of the client's financial situation, the agent can then provide an overview of the different types of mortgage options available. These can be broadly classified into fixed-rate mortgages, where the interest rate remains the same throughout the loan term, and adjustable-rate mortgages, where the interest rate can change based on market conditions. Within these categories, there are various products tailored for different needs, such as conventional loans, Federal Housing Administration (FHA) loans, Veteran Affairs (VA) loans, and United States Department of Agriculture (USDA) loans. The clients should be made aware of the benefits, limitations, and eligibility requirements of each type of loan to make an informed decision.

An important aspect to highlight during this discussion is the concept of down payments, interest rates, loan terms, and the potential impact of these elements on the monthly payments and overall loan cost. Agents can leverage mortgage calculators to illustrate how varying these factors can affect the client's financial commitment over the years. Clients should also be informed about the closing costs and any potential private mortgage insurance (PMI) expenses if their down payment is less than 20% of the property's price.

Real estate agents must also guide their clients through the pre-approval process. A mortgage pre-approval not only gives clients a clear idea of their borrowing capacity but also makes them more appealing to sellers, as it demonstrates their serious intent and financial ability to purchase the property.

In addition to traditional financing options, agents should also make their clients aware of alternatives such as seller financing, lease-to-own options, or local down payment assistance programs. For investment-oriented clients, hard money loans or real estate crowdfunding platforms might be relevant options.

However, throughout this process, it's crucial for agents to maintain their role as advisors and not lenders or financial advisors. While they should provide accurate information to help clients make informed decisions, they should also encourage clients to consult with a mortgage professional or financial advisor.

guiding clients through financing options is all about educating them, providing resources, and encouraging them to seek professional advice. It's a crucial part of an agent's role, making the path to homeownership or property investment less daunting and more accessible. This aspect of the agent's work can make a significant difference in the client's buying experience, further reinforcing their trust and potentially leading to long-term client relationships and referrals.

How do I help my clients get financing for their home purchase?

As a real estate agent, one of your most important roles is to help your clients navigate the complex process of securing financing for their home purchase. It's not just about finding the perfect home; it's also about helping your clients understand the financial implications and guide them through the often confusing and challenging mortgage process.

To start with, it's crucial to understand and explain the basics of home financing to your clients. Many first-time home buyers are unaware of the difference between pre-qualification, pre-approval, and mortgage commitment.

Pre-qualification is an informal determination by a lender or mortgage broker stating how much mortgage the borrower might be able to afford. It's based on a preliminary assessment of the borrower's income, assets, and debts. On the other hand, pre-approval is a more formal process where the lender verifies the borrower's financial information and credit rating, then determines precisely how much they're willing to lend. Lastly, a mortgage commitment is the final, binding agreement between the lender and borrower.

Your role as a real estate agent is to guide your clients through these stages. Encourage them to get pre-approval before house hunting, as this will give them an accurate idea of their budget and make them more attractive to sellers.

Networking with mortgage lenders and brokers can also prove to be advantageous. By establishing strong relationships with these professionals, you can refer your clients to them, knowing they will be in good hands. Additionally, these relationships will allow you to stay updated on the latest mortgage products, rates, and trends, which you can then pass on to your clients.

Understanding different loan types is also essential. From conventional loans to government-backed loans like the Federal Housing Administration (FHA), Veterans Affairs (VA), and the U.S. Department of Agriculture (USDA) loans, each comes with its own set of qualifications, benefits, and drawbacks. By understanding these options, you can help your clients choose the best one for their specific circumstances.

Moreover, as an agent, you should understand and explain the role of credit scores in securing a mortgage. A high credit score can lead to better mortgage rates and more options, while a low score can limit options and increase interest rates. Guide your clients on ways to improve their credit score, such as paying bills on time, reducing debt, and promptly correcting errors on their credit report.

Additionally, inform your clients about the importance of saving for a down payment. While certain loans allow for low or even zero down payment, saving a significant amount can lower the monthly payment and potentially eliminate the need for private mortgage insurance.

Lastly, be transparent about closing costs. Many home buyers are unaware of the additional costs involved in closing a home purchase, such as origination fees, title insurance, and inspection fees. Assist your clients in budgeting for these costs to avoid unpleasant surprises.

As a real estate agent, your role extends beyond showing homes and negotiating contracts. Helping your clients understand and navigate the process of securing home financing is an essential part of your job. By educating them about the process and guiding them through it, you can help them secure the financing they need to purchase their dream home.

How do you evaluate the financial risks and returns of a property investment?

When you embark on the journey of property investment, you are essentially becoming the steward of your financial future. One of the most critical aspects of this stewardship lies in your ability to evaluate the financial risks and returns of a property investment. This question delves into the methodologies and practical strategies to accurately assess these factors.

To begin with, it is fundamental to ascertain the potential return on investment (ROI). ROI is the ratio of the net income generated by the property to its purchase price. This simple formula provides a percentage that can be used to compare the profitability of different properties. But while ROI is a crucial indicator, it should not be the sole determinant of your investment decision.

The capitalization rate, or cap rate, is another essential factor to consider. The cap rate is the ratio of the net operating income of the property to its current market value. It provides a more accurate reflection of the property's performance because it incorporates changes in the property's value over time. A higher cap rate typically suggests a higher risk and potentially higher return.

Now, let's talk about the financial risks associated with property investment. The term 'risk' in real estate investment refers to the potential for financial loss. The first step to managing risk is identification. Some common risks include market risk (changes in market conditions), credit risk (the tenant's ability to pay rent), liquidity risk (the ability to sell the property when necessary), and operational risk (costs associated with managing the property).

After identifying the risks, the next step is to assess them. One method to do this is through a risk-return trade-off analysis. This involves comparing the potential return of an investment with its associated risks. Investments with higher expected returns are generally associated with higher risk. Therefore, as an investor, you must find a balance between the return you aim to achieve and the risk you are willing to tolerate.

The use of leverage, or borrowed capital, introduces another dimension of risk. While leverage can magnify your returns, it can also amplify your losses. It is, therefore, crucial to consider the cost of borrowing and your ability to service debt in your risk assessment.

Furthermore, conducting a thorough due diligence on the property is vital in mitigating risk. This process involves evaluating the property's condition, zoning regulations, potential environmental issues, and other factors that could impact the investment's profitability.

Lastly, remember that the market is cyclical. Economic indicators, such as the unemployment rate, GDP growth, and interest rates, influence the real estate market's performance. By understanding these indicators and their interplay, you can make informed predictions about future market trends and adjust your investment strategy accordingly.

evaluating the financial risks and returns of a property investment is not a simple task. However, by understanding and applying the principles and methodologies outlined in this question, you can make informed decisions that align with your investment goals and risk tolerance. Remember, real estate investment is not just about buying properties; it's about buying into a financial future that you can control.

In the next question, we will delve deeper into real estate market cycles and how to navigate them effectively. Until then, keep exploring, learning, and growing as a world-class real estate agent.

How do you work with mortgage lenders and brokers?

Understanding how to effectively work with mortgage lenders and brokers is a crucial component of becoming a successful real estate agent. These individuals play significant roles in the home-buying process, providing the necessary financing options for buyers. As a real estate agent, your role is not only to find the perfect property for your clients but also to guide them through the complex financial landscape.

Understanding the Role of Mortgage Lenders and Brokers

Mortgage lenders are financial institutions that lend money directly to the buyers to purchase homes. These can be banks, credit unions, or other financial entities. On the other hand, mortgage brokers are middlemen who act as a liaison between the lender and the buyer, helping the latter find a suitable mortgage product that fits their financial situation. While brokers can offer a range of options from different lenders, they do not lend the money directly.

Building Relationships with Lenders and Brokers

As a real estate agent, it's important to cultivate strong relationships with both mortgage lenders and brokers. This network can provide a wealth of information to help you guide clients through the financing aspect of their home purchase. Additionally, having a trusted lender or broker to refer clients to can make the process smoother and faster, improving your clients' overall experience.

Attend networking events, reach out directly for informational meetings, or ask for introductions from mutual contacts. Remember, this partnership should be mutually beneficial; refer clients to them, and they can potentially refer clients to you.

Understanding Mortgage Products

Mortgage lenders offer a variety of mortgage products with different interest rates, terms, and requirements. Understanding these options is essential to help your clients make informed choices. For instance, knowing the difference between a fixed-rate and adjustable-rate mortgage, or the pros and cons of a 15-year versus a 30-year term, can be invaluable when discussing financing options with your clients.

Assisting Your Clients

As a real estate agent, you can provide value by helping your clients navigate the mortgage process. Encourage them to seek pre-approval before house hunting, as this can give them a realistic understanding of what they can afford and demonstrate to sellers that they are serious buyers.

Remember that you are not a mortgage advisor, so always encourage clients to speak directly with a mortgage professional for specific advice. However, you can help with general advice such as explaining the importance of a good credit score, the impact of a down payment, and the additional costs involved in getting a mortgage, such as closing costs and property insurance.

Communicating Effectively

Effective communication between you, the buyer, and the mortgage lender or broker is key to a successful transaction. Be proactive in your communication, ensuring all parties are kept informed at each stage of the process. If issues arise, such as a delay in the mortgage approval or a lower than expected appraisal, quick and clear communication can help resolve them efficiently.

Working with mortgage lenders and brokers is an integral part of a real estate agent's role. By building strong relationships, understanding mortgage products, assisting your clients, and communicating effectively, you can help ensure a positive experience for your clients and a successful outcome for all parties involved. Remember, a well-informed client is a happy client, and a happy client is the best source of future business and referrals.

How do you explain the tax implications of buying and selling properties?

As a real estate agent, you need to have a fundamental understanding of the tax implications associated with buying and selling properties. Although you are not expected to substitute for a financial advisor or a tax consultant, your clients will appreciate your ability to provide them with a general overview of potential tax impacts on their real estate transactions. This knowledge will enable you to guide clients through the intricate process of buying and selling properties with an understanding of potential tax scenarios.

Let's start with buying properties. When your client buys a property, they may be subjected to certain taxes, such as stamp duty land tax, which is a tax on the purchase price of the property. The rate varies depending on the value of the property and the type of buyer (first-time buyer, home mover, or investor). Additionally, if the property is rented out, the rental income will be subject to income tax. However, certain expenses can be deducted from this income for tax purposes, including mortgage interest (subject to certain restrictions), maintenance costs, insurance, and agent's fees, among others.

Apart from these, property buyers should also be aware of the annual taxes associated with property ownership like local property taxes or council taxes, which are usually based on the valuation of the property. These taxes are used to fund local services such as garbage collection, street maintenance, and public safety services.

Moving onto selling properties, the principal tax implication is capital gains tax. This tax is applied on the profit that the seller makes from selling the property, which is the difference between the selling price and the original purchase price (after adjusting for certain costs and improvements). The rate of this tax can vary based on the seller's income tax bracket and the length of ownership. Importantly, if the property has been the seller's primary residence for at least two of the last five years, they may be eligible for a capital gains tax exclusion, which can significantly reduce their tax liability.

Additionally, a concept called 'depreciation recapture' applies when selling rental properties. This means that any depreciation deductions that were claimed on the property while it was rented out must be 'recaptured' or added back into the seller's income, and taxed at a specific rate.

Moreover, if a property is inherited, the beneficiaries may be liable for inheritance tax. However, the property's cost basis is 'stepped up' to the market value at the date of the previous owner's death, which potentially reduces the capital gains tax if the property is later sold.

Remember, tax laws are complex and vary from one jurisdiction to another. Therefore, it is important that you advise your clients to consult with a tax professional to understand the specific tax implications based on their individual circumstances.

Understanding the tax implications of buying and selling properties is crucial. Not only does it enhance your professionalism and credibility, but it also allows you to provide value-added service to your clients. By doing so, you can help clients navigate their real estate transactions more confidently and make more informed decisions, thus establishing a successful career in real estate.

How do you analyze market trends for real estate investment

opportunities?

As a real estate agent, understanding how to analyze market trends is an invaluable skill that can make or break your success in the industry. Real estate market trends can provide critical information about the current status of the market, its potential growth, and the best areas for investment. This understanding will not only allow you to make informed decisions but also help you advise your clients effectively.

Firstly, what is a market trend? In the realm of real estate, a market trend refers to the general direction of the market conditions prevailing in an area. They can be upward (rising prices), downward (falling prices), or stagnant (stable prices).

To analyze market trends, you need to consider various factors.

Property Prices

One of the most straightforward indicators of market trends is the change in property prices. Regularly monitoring the price of properties in your target area can give you a clear picture of the current market situation. If prices are increasing, the market is likely on an upward trend. Conversely, if prices are declining, the market might be on a downward trend.

Sales Volume

Sales volume refers to the number of properties sold within a specific period. A high sales volume indicates a strong market, while a low sales volume could mean a weak market. By comparing the sales volume over a span of months or years, you can determine whether the market is growing or declining.

Days on Market (DOM)

DOM is the number of days a property is listed on the market before it is sold. A shorter DOM indicates a seller's market where demand is high, and properties are selling quickly. On the other hand, a longer DOM suggests a buyer's market with lower demand.

Rental Yield

If you are interested in rental properties, the rental yield - the annual rent income divided by the property price - can be a significant indicator. A high rental yield means the property can generate a good return on investment.

Local Economy

The health of the local economy plays a vital role in real estate market trends. Factors like the unemployment rate, average income, population growth, and new businesses opening up can significantly impact the real estate market. If the local economy is strong, it's likely to attract more people, increasing demand for properties and potentially driving prices up.

Government Policies

Government policies, including tax laws, zoning regulations, and interest rates, can significantly affect real estate markets. For instance, a decrease in interest rates might spur more people to buy properties, thus increasing demand and potentially driving prices up.

Once you have gathered data on these factors, it's time to analyze them. Look for patterns and correlations. For example, if property prices are increasing alongside a rise in the local population and decline in unemployment rates, it might indicate an upward market trend.

However, remember that real estate markets are complex and influenced by numerous factors. Therefore, while this analysis can guide your decision-making, it should not be the sole determining factor. Other considerations, such as your client's specific needs and financial situation, should also come into play.

Analyzing real estate market trends is a multi-faceted process that requires thorough research and a comprehensive understanding of various factors. As a real estate agent aspiring to be world-class, mastering this skill can significantly enhance your ability to spot investment opportunities and guide your clients to success.

10 TECHNOLOGY IN REAL ESTATE

How do you leverage technology in your work as a real estate agent?

The Technological Leverage: A Boon for Modern Real Estate Agents
In the technologically driven world of the 21st century, the real estate sector, much like every other industry, has had to adapt and evolve. As a real estate agent, leveraging technology is not just a bonus, but it is integral to keep up with the fast-paced market, meet customer expectations, and stand out amongst competitors. Technology in real estate, commonly referred to as PropTech (Property Technology), revolutionizes the way real estate agents approach their work.

The first aspect of technology leveraged in real estate involves database and customer relationship management (CRM) systems. These software platforms organize and streamline contacts, property listings, appointments, transactions, and follow-ups. A well-managed database can significantly improve efficiency, ensuring that no potential leads or vital tasks slip through the cracks. Additionally, CRM systems can automate various tasks such as sending emails, texts, or notifications, allowing the agent to focus on more critical, high-value tasks.

Next comes the area of property listings and marketing. Online platforms have made it easier for agents to reach a global audience. The likes of Zillow, Realtor.com, and Trulia offer vast databases of properties for sale or rent, bringing together buyers, sellers, and agents on a single platform. This expansive reach was unimaginable a couple of decades back. In addition, social media platforms like Facebook, Instagram, LinkedIn, and Twitter provide an excellent medium to showcase properties visually and reach potential clients.

In the era of Covid-19 and beyond, virtual tours have become essential. Using technologies like 3D imaging, drone photography, and virtual reality, agents can provide potential buyers with immersive experiences of properties from the comfort of their homes. These tools not only save time and resources but also widen the geographical scope of potential buyers.

The use of mobile technology is another aspect that cannot be overlooked. The ability to access information, communicate, and manage transactions on-the-go is crucial in a time-sensitive business like real estate. There are numerous apps designed to help agents with property searches, comparables, mortgage calculators, e-signatures, and even virtual staging.

Finally, the advent of artificial intelligence (AI) and machine learning in the real estate industry marks a new era. AI can help predict market trends, making the property valuation process more accurate. It also improves lead generation and conversion through predictive analytics and automated follow-ups. Machine learning algorithms can analyze patterns and trends from vast amounts of data to provide valuable insights into customer behavior, preferences, and the likelihood of transaction closure.

Leveraging technology is no longer an option but a necessity in the dynamic field of real estate. It enhances efficiency, broadens reach, offers convenience, and drives data-driven decision-making. However, technology should complement, not replace, the human touch, which is central to real estate transactions. Therefore, striking the right balance between using technology and maintaining personal relationships is the key to being a successful real estate agent in the digital age.

Why is it important to run your business using real estate software and digital tools?

To become a world-class real estate agent, it is essential to become highly familiar with and proficient in the use of real estate software and digital tools. These tools can greatly enhance your productivity, effectiveness, and competitiveness in the fast-paced and ever-evolving real estate industry. In this question, we will delve into the importance of these tools, the types of software and digital tools available, and how best to utilize them.

These technological assets can help you automate and streamline many aspects of your work, from property management, client communication, to market analysis, and much more. They can save you substantial amount of time and effort, enabling you to focus more on building relationships with your clients and closing deals. Moreover, they can provide you with valuable insights into the real estate market and your clients, helping you make more informed and strategic decisions.

There are various types of real estate software and digital tools available, each designed to serve different purposes.

CRM Software
Customer Relationship Management (CRM) software is designed to help you manage your interactions with current and potential clients. A good CRM system can help you keep track of your clients' preferences, needs, and history, enhancing your ability to cater to them effectively and personally. Examples of popular CRM software for real estate agents include Zoho CRM, Pipedrive, and HubSpot CRM.

Property Management Software
This type of software helps you manage properties, tenants, and related transactions. It can automate various tasks such as rent collection, maintenance requests, and lease management. Examples include Propertyware, AppFolio, and Buildium.

MLS Software
Multiple Listing Service (MLS) software provides access to a comprehensive database of property listings. It's crucial for finding properties that meet your clients' criteria and for listing your own properties. Examples include Matrix, Flexmls, and Rapattoni.

Market Analysis Software
This software helps you analyze and understand the real estate market trends. It can provide insights into property values, rental rates, neighborhood demographics, and more. Examples include Zillow, Trulia, and Realtors Property Resource (RPR).

Digital Marketing Tools
These tools can help you promote your properties and services online. They can help you create and manage social media campaigns, email marketing campaigns, and websites. Examples include MailChimp for email marketing, Hootsuite for social media management, and WordPress for website creation and management.

It's not enough to just know about these tools; you need to become proficient in using them. This requires continuous learning and practice. You can take advantage of various online resources to learn about these tools, such as tutorials, webinars, and online courses. You can also attend industry conferences and workshops, where you can learn from experts and peers.

Technology is not a substitute for essential real estate skills like negotiation, communication, and customer service. However, mastering real estate software and digital tools can greatly enhance these skills and give you a significant edge in the industry. So, keep learning, keep practicing, and strive to become a tech-savvy real estate agent.

How do you use digital platforms for property listings?

In today's high-tech world, the importance of leveraging digital platforms to list properties effectively cannot be overstated. As a real estate agent, you must adapt to the digital era and use these platforms to your advantage to reach a wider audience, provide comprehensive property information, and ultimately close successful deals.

To start with, let's understand what digital platforms for property listings are. These are web-based applications or websites where real estate agents can list properties they are selling or renting. Examples include Zillow, Realtor.com, Trulia, and many others. These platforms allow you to upload photos, videos, and detailed descriptions of the property to attract potential buyers.

The first step in using digital platforms for property listings is to choose the right platform. Not all platforms are created equal. Some cater to high-end luxury properties, while others are best for budget-friendly homes or rentals. Research each platform to determine which one is the best fit for your property type, target market, and location. Some platforms have more traffic than others, so consider the potential reach of each site.

Once you have selected the platform, you need to create a compelling property listing. The key elements of a great listing include high-quality photos, a detailed description, and accurate property information.

Photographs are the first thing potential buyers see, and they can either make or break your listing. Ensure you use high-resolution images that highlight the best features of the property. If possible, hire a professional real estate photographer. They have the skill and experience to capture a property in its best light, both literally and figuratively. Additionally, consider adding a virtual tour or video walkthrough of the property.

When writing the property description, be as detailed as possible. Highlight the unique features of the property, its location, and any recent upgrades or improvements. A well-written description can paint a picture in the buyer's mind and spark their interest in viewing the property.

Accurate property information is also crucial. Ensure you provide the correct details about the property's square footage, number of bedrooms and bathrooms, lot size, and any additional amenities like a swimming pool or a basement. Incorrect or misleading information can lead to potential legal issues and damage your reputation as a real estate agent.

Once your listing is live, you need to monitor it closely. Respond promptly to inquiries and comments. This not only shows potential buyers that you are professional and reliable, but also that you value their interest.

Another key aspect of using digital platforms is promoting your listings through social media. Platforms like Facebook, Instagram, and LinkedIn allow you to reach a wider audience and engage with potential buyers in a more personal way. Ensure you share your listings on your social media accounts and encourage your followers to share them as well.

Finally, always keep track of your listings' performance. Most digital platforms provide analytics that show how many people viewed your listing, how many inquiries you received, and other useful information. This data can help you understand what works and what doesn't, allowing you to tweak your approach and improve your listings.

Using digital platforms for property listings is an essential skill for any world-class real estate agent. It allows you to reach a wider audience, provide detailed property information, and interact with potential buyers in an efficient and effective way. By mastering this skill, you can increase your chances of closing successful deals and advancing your real estate career.

How do you stay updated on technological advancements in the real estate industry?

As a real estate agent, your success is not solely dependent on your ability to close deals, but also on your ability to adapt to new trends, especially those that are technology-driven. The real estate industry, like many other sectors, is constantly evolving due to technological advancements. Staying updated on these changes is no longer optional; it has become a necessity. In this section, we will discuss various ways to stay informed about technological advancements in the real estate industry.

Subscribe to Real Estate Tech Newsletters
Many companies and organizations in the real estate industry publish newsletters that are rich in content about the latest tech trends. These newsletters provide insights into new software, tools, and platforms that can help real estate agents improve their efficiency, reach, and effectiveness. Some recommended newsletters include Inman, Propmodo, Tech Estate Today, and CREtech.

Attend Tech-Based Real Estate Conferences
Conferences offer an excellent opportunity to learn about innovative technologies directly from the experts. They also provide a platform to network with industry peers and tech providers. Key conferences to consider include the Realcomm Conference Group, which focuses on technology, automation, and innovation for the industry, and the National Association of REALTORS® Conference & Expo, which features numerous tech-based sessions.

Join Online Forums and Discussion Groups
Online platforms like LinkedIn, Reddit, and Quora host numerous real estate groups where members share insights about the latest technologies in the industry. Being part of such communities can offer firsthand information and practical insights about implementing these technologies.

Participate in Webinars and Online Courses
Many tech companies and real estate organizations conduct webinars and online courses to educate industry professionals about new technologies. Websites like Coursera, Udemy, and Khan Academy also offer courses on real estate technology.

Follow Tech and Real Estate Blogs

Blogs are another great source of information. They provide in-depth analysis and reviews about the latest tools and technologies. Some of the blogs to follow include GeekEstate, PropTech, and the Zillow Tech Blog.

Engage with PropTech Startups

PropTech, a term that refers to businesses using technology to refine, improve or reinvent the services we rely on in the property industry, is a rapidly growing field. By engaging with PropTech startups, agents can get early access to innovative solutions, stay ahead of their competition, and provide better services to their clients.

Use Social Media

Platforms such as Twitter and Facebook are not just for social networking. Many tech companies, industry experts, and fellow real estate professionals share valuable information about the latest trends and technologies in real estate on these platforms. Following the right people and companies can keep you updated.

Experiment with New Tools

Lastly, the best way to understand a new technology is to use it. Free trials are often available, allowing you to evaluate a tool's effectiveness before making a commitment. This hands-on approach can provide a deeper understanding of how specific technologies can benefit your business.

Staying updated on technological advancements in the real estate industry requires a proactive approach and a commitment to continuous learning. Embracing technology can significantly enhance the way you do business, offering improved efficiency, greater reach, and superior service to your clients. Remember, in an industry as competitive as real estate, those who leverage technology will lead the pack.

How has technology transformed the real estate profession?

In the rapidly evolving world of technology, the real estate industry has experienced transformative changes that have reshaped the way real estate agents conduct business, interact with clients, and manage properties. The advent of digital platforms, artificial intelligence, and augmented reality, among others, have created a new landscape for real estate professionals, enhancing efficiency, convenience, and profitability.

One of the most significant technological advancements is the emergence of online real estate platforms. Websites and applications such as Zillow, Realtor.com, and Trulia have made property listings accessible to a global audience. Agents can now reach potential buyers and renters at a scale that was previously unimaginable. These platforms not only provide agents with a vast marketplace but also offer tools for tracking market trends, pricing properties, and scheduling virtual tours.

Further, the integration of big data and artificial intelligence (AI) into real estate has revolutionized the decision-making process. Agents can now use predictive analytics to forecast market trends, determine property values, and identify potential investment opportunities. AI has also facilitated the automation of various tasks such as lead generation and client management, freeing up time for agents to focus on more complex aspects of their work.

Another significant innovation is the use of virtual and augmented reality (VR and AR). These technologies have transformed the way properties are showcased, making it possible for prospective buyers and renters to take virtual tours of properties from anywhere in the world. This not only saves time and resources but also allows clients to explore properties in detail, enhancing their decision-making process.

Additionally, technology has also improved communication and collaboration in the real estate industry. Tools like video conferencing and cloud-based software have made it easy for agents to collaborate with clients, colleagues, and other stakeholders in real-time, regardless of their location. This has significantly improved service delivery, client satisfaction, and overall productivity.

Moreover, the rise of proptech - technology designed specifically for the property market - has made property management more efficient. Agents can now use software to manage rental properties, track maintenance requests, and collect rent electronically. This has made property management more streamlined and less time-consuming, allowing agents to manage more properties effectively.

However, as much as technology has transformed the real estate profession, it is essential to note that it has also brought about new challenges. The digital landscape is often marked by issues such as data privacy and cybersecurity. As such, real estate professionals must equip themselves with knowledge and skills to navigate these challenges effectively. They must understand how to protect their digital assets and use technology responsibly to maintain trust and credibility with their clients.

There is no doubt that technology has dramatically transformed the real estate profession. It has brought about efficiencies, expanded markets, enhanced decision-making, and improved client interactions. However, to fully harness the benefits of these advancements, real estate professionals need to continuously adapt and innovate. They must stay abreast with the latest technologies, invest in digital skills, and adopt a forward-thinking approach. As the technological landscape continues to evolve, so too will the possibilities for the real estate industry. The future of real estate is undeniably digital, and it is exciting to imagine what the next wave of technological innovation will bring to this dynamic profession.

11 CAREER DEVELOPMENT AND GROWTH

How do you set your career goals as a real estate agent?

As you embark upon your journey to become a world-class real estate agent, it's imperative to set clear and achievable career goals. These goals will provide a roadmap for your journey, defining your destination and the steps needed to get there.

First, it's essential to understand that career goals are different from day-to-day objectives. Career goals are the big picture items that represent what you want to accomplish in your profession. They are the milestones that you aim to achieve over the course of your career, and they require both long-term planning and consistent effort.

Define Your Vision
Before you can set specific career goals, you must first define your vision. A vision is a broad, inspiring image of the future you're aiming to create. For instance, do you want to become the top-selling agent in your city? Or perhaps you aim to specialize in luxury properties, or to build a successful real estate agency of your own. Whatever your vision, it should be something that motivates and excites you.

Set SMART Goals
Once you have a clear vision, you can start to set specific goals. To be effective, your goals should be SMART: Specific, Measurable, Achievable, Relevant, and Time-bound.

For instance, rather than setting a goal to "sell more houses," a SMART goal would be to "sell 20% more houses in the next quarter compared to the previous one." This goal is specific (sell 20% more houses), measurable (you can track the number of houses you sell), achievable (assuming you're

106

willing to put in the required effort), relevant (it directly contributes to your career success), and time-bound (you have a set timeframe of one quarter).

Long-Term and Short-Term Goals

Your career goals as a real estate agent should include both long-term and short-term objectives. Long-term goals usually span several years and are directly tied to your vision. They give you a direction and a sense of purpose.

Short-term goals, on the other hand, are the steps you need to take to achieve your long-term goals. They typically range from several weeks to a year and should be reviewed and updated regularly.

For example, if your long-term goal is to become the top-selling agent in your city, you might set short-term goals to increase your client base, improve your sales techniques, or expand your professional network.

Regular Review and Adjustment

Setting career goals isn't a one-time task. As you progress in your career and as circumstances change, your goals should be reviewed and adjusted accordingly. Regular review allows you to track your progress, celebrate your achievements, and identify areas for improvement. It also allows you to adjust your goals as needed, ensuring that they remain relevant and achievable.

Remain Resilient and Persistent

Lastly, remember that the journey to becoming a world-class real estate agent is a marathon, not a sprint. There will be obstacles and setbacks along the way, but it's your resilience and persistence that will carry you through. Stay focused on your goals, and don't let temporary setbacks discourage you.

setting clear and achievable career goals is a vital step in becoming a successful real estate agent. By defining your vision, setting SMART goals, balancing long-term and short-term objectives, regularly reviewing and adjusting your goals, and staying resilient and persistent, you can create a roadmap for your journey to success in the real estate industry.

What are your long-term plans in the real estate industry?

Having a clear and well-considered long-term plan is crucial for any career, but perhaps more so in real estate. The industry is competitive, sometimes volatile, and requires consistent dedication and hard work. However, with the right strategy and long-term vision, you can become a world-class real estate agent, capable of navigating and thriving in any market.

The first step in charting your long-term plans in real estate is to identify your ultimate goal. What is it that you want to achieve? Do you want to be a top sales agent, a respected broker, or maybe the owner of your own real estate agency? Each of these goals will require a different set of skills and a distinct roadmap. It's essential to have clarity about your final destination from the outset, as it will help guide your decisions and strategies along the way.

Once you've established your ultimate goal, it's time to start planning the steps you need to take to get there. Think of this as your career ladder, with each rung representing a new skill, experience, or achievement you need to reach your goal. For example, if you aspire to own a real estate agency, you might start as a sales agent, move up to a broker, then branch manager, before finally opening your own firm. Each step on this ladder will provide valuable experience and knowledge that will prepare you for your end goal.

In addition to climbing the career ladder, consider what skills and knowledge you need to acquire. The real estate industry is multifaceted, requiring a broad range of skills including negotiation, marketing, customer service, financial analysis, and legal knowledge. Identify which of these skills you need to improve or learn and make a plan to do so. This could involve attending seminars, courses or finding a mentor in the industry.

Moreover, consider the market trends and changes in the industry. Real estate, like any other industry, evolves over time. The rise of online property platforms, for example, has dramatically changed how real estate transactions are conducted. As part of your long-term plan, you should continuously be aware of these changes and adapt accordingly. Make it a part of your routine to stay updated with industry news and trends.

Another crucial aspect of your long-term plan is networking. Making connections in the real estate industry can lead to partnerships, mentorship opportunities, and referrals. Attend industry events, join real estate associations, and make a habit of introducing yourself to new people. Networking is a long-term investment that can pay significant dividends in your career.

Finally, remember that success in real estate does not come overnight. It requires patience, resilience, and a lot of hard work. There will be challenges, setbacks, and even failures along the way. But with a well-thought-out long-term plan, you can navigate these obstacles and stay on course.

Your long-term plans in the real estate industry should be a combination of your ultimate career goal, the career steps you need to take, the skills and knowledge you need to acquire, market trends, networking, and a lot of patience and hard work. Keep your vision in mind, but be prepared to adapt and grow as you progress. The path to becoming a world-class real estate agent is not a straight line, but with the right plan and mindset, it's a journey that can be incredibly rewarding.

How do you handle career challenges and setbacks?

In your journey towards becoming a world-class real estate agent, you will inevitably face a myriad of career challenges and setbacks. The real estate industry is a fluctuating market, and no matter how much knowledge you accumulate or how well you prepare, there will be times when things do not go as planned. It is essential to understand that these obstacles are not indicative of your aptitude or potential. Instead, they represent opportunities for growth and evolution.

Firstly, it's crucial to embrace a positive mindset. Any career, not just real estate, is bound to come with its share of disappointments and challenges. It's how you confront these situations that will significantly influence your career trajectory. Seeing challenges as opportunities for learning and growth can fundamentally shift your perspective and open up new pathways for success. This shift in mindset may not come naturally, but it's a valuable tool that can help you navigate through an often unpredictable real estate market.

When setbacks occur, take a step back and analyze the situation objectively. What led to the setback? What could have been done differently? This kind of self-assessment is not about assigning blame but identifying areas for improvement. By understanding the factors that contributed to the setback, you can begin to develop strategies to avoid similar situations in the future.

Next, it's essential to maintain resilience. The real estate market is dynamic and constantly changing. There will be high and low periods, and during these times, your resilience is what will keep you moving forward. Resilience doesn't mean ignoring the difficulties or pretending they don't exist. Instead, it's about acknowledging the challenge, understanding that it's part of the journey, and then finding ways to move forward in the face of adversity.

Building a support network is another key aspect of managing career challenges and setbacks. This network can be comprised of mentors, colleagues, friends, or family who can provide advice, share their own experiences, and offer emotional support. Surrounding yourself with positive and supportive people can significantly help you navigate through difficult times.

Continuing education and personal development should also be at the forefront of your strategy to handle career challenges. The real estate industry is continually evolving, and staying up-to-date on the latest trends, regulations, and market conditions is paramount to your success. Regularly attending seminars, webinars, and courses not only equips you with the knowledge to tackle challenges head-on but also shows potential clients and peers your commitment to your profession.

Remember that setbacks are temporary. While it may feel at the moment like a significant blow, with time and persistence, you'll get back on track. Setbacks should not define you or your career. Instead, they should serve as lessons that shape you into a better, more experienced real estate agent.

Confronting and overcoming challenges and setbacks is an integral part of your journey to becoming a top real estate agent. By adopting a positive mindset, analyzing setbacks, maintaining resilience, building a support network, pursuing continuous learning, and understanding the temporary nature of setbacks, you equip yourself with the tools needed to navigate and thrive in the ever-changing real estate industry. This process will not only make you a better professional but also a stronger, more resilient individual.

How do you seek feedback and learn from your mistakes?

In the dynamic world of real estate, there is no room for complacency. Constant self-improvement is key to becoming a world-class real estate agent. This necessitates the importance of seeking feedback and learning from one's mistakes.

The first step in seeking feedback is to understand that it is not a critique of you as an individual, but rather an opportunity for growth and personal development. By adopting a mindset that views feedback as a positive, you can use it to fine-tune your skills, expand your knowledge, and improve your performance. Remember, the purpose of feedback is to help you become a better agent.

Reach out to your clients, peers, mentors, and even your competitors for feedback. With clients, you can ask for feedback at the end of a transaction or a few months after. A simple phone call or email asking for their thoughts on your service can provide valuable insights. This can be structured in a way that they can provide both positive feedback and areas for improvement.

Peers and mentors can provide a different perspective, perhaps pointing out habits or behaviors you may not even be aware of. They can also provide advice on how to improve. Competitors can be a great source of feedback too. By observing their practices and successes, you can learn what works well and what doesn't in the industry.

Consider using feedback tools and platforms for a more organized approach. Online surveys, for example, can be used to collect feedback from clients. These can be made anonymous to encourage honesty. Social media platforms also provide an avenue for feedback. Monitor your online presence, respond to comments, and take note of recurring praises or complaints.

Once you have gathered feedback, it is crucial to act on it. This is where learning from your mistakes comes into play. Reflect on the feedback you've received and identify the common themes. Are there specific areas where you consistently receive negative feedback? These are your areas of weakness and where you should focus your improvement efforts.

Take ownership of your mistakes. It's natural to feel defensive when our shortcomings are pointed out, but it's important to resist this urge. Accept your mistakes, learn from them, and use the experience to grow. For example, if a client felt that you didn't communicate enough during the sale process, instead of explaining why you didn't, acknowledge their feelings, apologize, and plan how you can improve your communication in future transactions.

Mistakes are valuable learning opportunities. They highlight your weaknesses and provide a clear path to improvement. If you didn't fully understand a contract and it cost your client, use this as a prompt to enhance your knowledge in that area. If a marketing strategy didn't work as expected, analyze why it failed and what could be done differently next time.

Finally, always strive for continuous improvement. The real estate market is ever-changing, and so should you be. Regularly seek feedback, keep learning from your mistakes, and continuously enhance your skills and knowledge. This ongoing cycle of feedback and improvement will not only make you a better agent, but it will also set you apart as a true professional in the field.

Seeking feedback and learning from mistakes are not just about recovering from failures; they're about turning those failures into stepping stones towards success. This process of self-improvement plays a pivotal role in your journey to becoming a world-class real estate agent.

How do you maintain work-life balance in this demanding profession?

As a real estate agent, you are essentially an entrepreneur. You have immense flexibility in managing your time, but this freedom can also lead you down the path of overwork and burnout. Maintaining a healthy work-life balance in this demanding profession is crucial for your long-term success and well-being. This question offers practical tips on how you can achieve this.

First and foremost, it is essential to understand that work-life balance doesn't necessarily mean an equal division of hours between work and personal life. It refers to a harmonious blend where neither aspect feels neglected. As a real estate agent, there will be times when work demands will be high, such as when closing a deal, and other times when it may be quieter, allowing you to take a step back and recharge.

Set clear boundaries and stick to them. Real estate is a business that operates beyond the typical 9-to-5 hours, including evenings and weekends. However, it doesn't mean you should be available 24/Clearly communicate your working hours to your clients and avoid responding to non-urgent emails or calls during your off-hours. This boundary setting is crucial for your mental health and prevents burnout.

Time management is a key skill in achieving work-life balance. Prioritize your tasks and focus on activities that generate the highest return on investment. Utilize technology to automate repetitive tasks like email follow-ups or appointment scheduling. Delegate non-core tasks, if possible, to an assistant or a virtual assistant. This will free up your time to focus on revenue-generating activities and also on your personal life.

Take advantage of the flexibility that real estate offers. If you are not a morning person, schedule your appointments later in the day. If you prefer to take Wednesdays off to spend with your family, block that time off in your calendar. Use this flexibility to create a schedule that suits your lifestyle and helps you perform at your best.

Remember, it is okay to say no. As real estate agents, we often feel the need to seize every opportunity that comes our way. However, taking on too much can lead to stress and lower the quality of your work. Be selective and commit to deals that align with your business goals and personal values.

Invest in self-care. Regular exercise, a healthy diet, and adequate sleep are not luxuries but necessities. These not only keep you physically healthy but also boost your mood and mental clarity, making you more effective in your work. Make time for activities you enjoy outside of work. It could be reading, hiking, painting, or simply spending time with loved ones. These activities help you relax and recharge, enhancing your productivity when you return to work.

Lastly, keep your long-term goals in perspective. It's easy to get caught up in the daily grind and lose sight of why you embarked on this career path. Regularly review your goals and evaluate your progress. If your current work habits are not sustainable or don't align with your goals, it may be time to make some changes.

Achieving a healthy work-life balance as a real estate agent is not a one-size-fits-all formula. It requires self-awareness, discipline, and continuous adjustments. Remember, your career is a marathon, not a sprint. Prioritizing your well-being and personal life will not only make you a happier individual but also a more successful real estate agent in the long run.

How do I become a top performer in the real estate industry?

The road to becoming a top performer in the real estate industry is not paved overnight. It requires a mixture of skills, knowledge, hard work, and a bit of luck. This question aims to provide a roadmap to help you navigate the path to becoming a world-class real estate agent.

Expert Knowledge

One of the most crucial attributes of a high-flying real estate agent is having a comprehensive understanding of the market. This includes knowledge of the local and national real estate landscape, current trends, market analysis, and financial factors affecting the real estate industry. A solid understanding of real estate law and contracts is equally vital. This knowledge serves as the foundation of your career. It's important to note that learning is a lifelong process. Attend seminars, workshops, and training sessions to continually update your knowledge base.

Building a Strong Network

Networking is a critical part of the real estate industry. A robust network can provide a continual stream of referrals, which can be a significant source of business. Networking events, community activities, real estate seminars, and social media platforms can be excellent places to connect with potential clients, industry professionals, and influencers. Remember, your network should not only be extensive but also well-maintained. Regular follow-ups and maintaining a positive relationship with your contacts are crucial.

Exceptional Customer Service

High performing real estate agents understand that they are in the service industry. Providing exceptional customer service can set you apart from the competition. This involves listening to your clients, understanding their needs and wants, and responding appropriately. Be proactive in communication, provide timely responses, and always keep your clients' best interests at heart. Remember, a satisfied client can be a source of repeat business and referrals.

Embrace Technology

In today's age, technology plays a significant role in the real estate industry. It not only helps in streamlining operations but also in reaching out to a larger audience. Learn to use real estate software and applications for market analysis, property listings, customer relationship management, and virtual tours. Utilize social media platforms for marketing and networking. Having a strong online presence can enhance your brand visibility and credibility.

Ethical Practices

Adherence to ethical practices is paramount in the real estate industry. This involves honesty, integrity, and transparency in all your dealings. Misrepresentation or fraudulent activities can not only tarnish your reputation but also lead to legal issues. Understand and abide by the National Association of Realtors (NAR) Code of Ethics.

Persistence and Resilience

The real estate industry is highly competitive and can be unpredictable. Deals can fall through at the last minute, markets can fluctuate, and clients can be difficult. Success often comes to those who show resilience in the face of adversity and persist despite challenges. It is essential to stay motivated, focused, and strive for your goals relentlessly.

Personal Branding

Top real estate agents have a strong personal brand. They are not just selling properties; they are selling themselves, their expertise, and their services. Develop a unique selling proposition (USP) that sets you apart from the competition. Use this USP in all your marketing materials and communication.

Becoming a top performer in the real estate industry is not an easy task. It requires a combination of the right skills, knowledge, attitude, and effort. However, with commitment, perseverance, and a customer-centric approach, you can certainly rise to the top and become a world-class real estate agent. Remember, success is a journey, not a destination. Keep learning, keep improving, and keep pushing your limits.

12 ADVANCED REAL ESTATE SCENARIOS AND CASE STUDIES

What do you do when a property's appraisal comes in lower than the selling price?

In the world of real estate transactions, one of the most challenging situations you may encounter as an agent is when a property's appraisal comes in lower than the selling price. This situation can be a significant impediment to closing a deal, but a competent real estate agent should be prepared to navigate this process with skill and diplomacy. Here are several strategies to handle this situation effectively.

First, it's crucial to understand why the appraisal might come in lower than the selling price. Several factors could contribute to this, such as recent comparable sales, the overall condition of the property, or even the appraiser's lack of local market knowledge. As an agent, you should review the appraisal report thoroughly to identify any discrepancies or inaccuracies. After understanding the reason behind the low appraisal, you have several options:

Challenge the Appraisal
If you believe there are errors in the appraisal report or that the appraiser may not have considered all relevant information, you can challenge the appraisal. This process involves writing a detailed letter to the lender explaining why you think the appraisal is incorrect, along with any supporting documents such as recent comparable sales or data about the neighborhood. However, keep in mind that this option can be time-consuming and doesn't always result in a higher appraisal.

Negotiate with the Buyer
If challenging the appraisal does not seem feasible or if it fails, you can

negotiate with the buyer. They might agree to pay the difference between the appraisal and the selling price, especially if they are highly motivated to purchase the property. However, this often depends on whether the buyer has the financial capacity and willingness to pay more than the appraised value.

Adjust the Selling Price

Another option is to lower the selling price to match the appraisal value. While this might not be the most attractive option for the seller, it can be a practical solution if the deal needs to be closed quickly. It's your job as an agent to advise your seller on the pros and cons of this decision.

Order a Second Appraisal

If you strongly disagree with the appraisal and the buyer is willing, you can order a second appraisal. This option can be costly and time-consuming, but it could result in a higher valuation if the first appraiser missed key property features or comparable sales.

Cancel the Transaction

If all else fails and the buyer and seller cannot agree on how to proceed, the transaction may need to be cancelled. This is typically a last resort option, as it doesn't benefit any party involved.

In all these scenarios, it's important to maintain open and respectful communication between all parties involved, including the buyer, seller, lender, and appraiser. As a real estate agent, you are a facilitator in this process. Your role is to help your clients navigate these difficult situations, advocate for their interests, and ultimately, help them make decisions that are in their best financial interest.

A low property appraisal doesn't have to be a deal-breaker. With your expertise and guidance, you can turn this challenging situation into an opportunity for problem-solving and negotiation. This not only helps to close the deal but also strengthens your reputation as a competent and reliable real estate agent.

How would you negotiate a deal with a seller who is unrealistic about their property's value?

One of the most challenging aspects of real estate is negotiating with sellers who have an inflated perception of their property's value. As a real estate agent, your job is not just to sell properties but also to guide your clients to make rational, informed decisions that are beneficial for them. This question will provide strategies on how to navigate negotiations with unrealistic sellers.

Firstly, you must understand why a seller might have an unrealistic price in mind. It could be emotional attachment, lack of market knowledge, or simply the desire to make a large profit. Understanding the reason behind the seller's unrealistic expectations can help you tailor your approach accordingly.

Start with Empathy
Begin your conversation on a positive note, acknowledging the seller's emotional connection to the property. Empathize with their attachment and allow them to express their feelings about the house. This approach makes them feel understood and sets a cooperative tone for the negotiations.

Educate the Seller
Once you've established rapport, it's time to educate the seller about the current market situation. As an expert in the field, you should have accurate, up-to-date data on hand, such as recent sales of comparable properties, market trends, and buyer expectations.

Use visual aids like charts, graphs, and pictures to convey this information effectively. Remember, numbers and data are more convincing than opinions. This will help the seller understand the price at which similar properties are selling and the factors driving those sales.

Honesty is Key
Be honest but respectful when discussing the property's shortcomings. Avoid using confrontational language. Instead, focus on how these shortcomings could affect the prospective buyers' perceptions and, in turn, the property's market value.

For example, instead of saying, "The kitchen is outdated," you could say, "New buyers might see the kitchen as a potential renovation project, which could affect their willingness to pay the asking price." This way, you're not criticizing the property but rather pointing out how others might perceive it.
Reiterate Your Role: Remind the seller that you both have the same goal - to sell the property at the best possible price. Reiterate that your role is to guide and support them through this process, providing expert advice based

on your knowledge and experience.

Provide a Plan

If the seller remains resistant to adjust the price, propose a marketing plan that aims to achieve the highest possible price. This could include professional photography, staging, open houses, and strategic advertising. Ensure the seller understands that while you will strive to obtain the highest price, the market will ultimately dictate the final selling price.

Negotiate Terms

If the seller still insists on an unrealistic price, you may consider negotiating terms instead. For example, you could agree to list at the seller's price but include a clause in your agreement that if the property doesn't sell within a certain period or there's minimal buyer interest, the seller agrees to reduce the price to a more realistic figure.

Dealing with unrealistic sellers requires patience, diplomacy, and excellent communication skills. It can be a delicate balancing act between managing the seller's expectations and striving to achieve the best possible outcome for them. With the right approach, you can guide the seller towards a more realistic understanding of their property's value. This will not only help close the deal more quickly but also solidify your reputation as a reliable, successful real estate agent.

How would you deal with a buyer who keeps changing their mind about the properties they want?

When you work in real estate, you are likely to encounter a variety of client personalities. Among these, one of the most challenging can be the indecisive buyer. This is the individual who keeps changing their mind about the properties they wish to buy, leaving you in a constant state of flux. While this can be frustrating, there are effective strategies for managing such situations and helping your buyer arrive at a decision they will be happy with.

First and foremost, it is crucial to establish clear and open communication. The key to understanding your client's needs and wants is to listen carefully to what they are saying and not saying. This may involve asking probing questions to uncover their true desires and requirements in a property. For instance, if they seem uncertain, ask them about their lifestyle, their family's needs, their preferred neighborhoods, and their budget, among other things. The answers to these questions should give you a clear picture of what they are looking for and help you guide them towards a suitable property.

Next, patience is a virtue that every real estate agent must have in abundance. An indecisive buyer can test this virtue, but remember that buying a property is a significant life decision. Most people do not take it lightly. Therefore, while you may feel the urge to rush them, resist it. Instead, provide them with the time and space they need to make their decision.

While patience is essential, it's also critical not to let an indecisive buyer drag on the property search indefinitely. It's here that your skills as a guide and advisor come into play. You must gently, but firmly, steer them towards making a decision. This may involve showing them a property multiple times, walking them through the pros and cons, or even seeking the opinion of a third party, like a home inspector, to provide an unbiased view of the property's condition.

Another effective strategy is to leverage the power of comparison. If your client is torn between two or more properties, create a detailed comparison chart highlighting the features, pros, and cons of each property. This visual aid can help simplify the decision-making process for them.

It's also vital to manage expectations. Some buyers have a dream home in mind that may not exist within their budget. Help them understand the reality of the market and guide them to prioritize their needs. The ultimate goal is to find a property that ticks most, if not all, of their boxes.

Remember, each client is unique, and what works for one may not work for another. Some buyers may need more reassurance, while others may need a nudge to take action. As a real estate agent, your goal is to adapt your approach to meet the client's needs, even if that means dealing with a bit of indecisiveness.

Lastly, remember that dealing with an indecisive buyer can be a learning experience. It can help you hone your skills as a real estate agent and teach you how to handle a wide range of client personalities. So, while it may be challenging, it can also be a valuable part of your journey towards becoming a world-class real estate agent.

Dealing with an indecisive buyer requires a combination of patience, excellent communication, market knowledge, and strategic guidance. By employing these tactics, you can navigate the complexities of an indecisive buyer and guide them towards making a decision that they will be satisfied with.

What strategies would you use to sell a property that's been on the market for a long time?

In the dynamic world of real estate, there are times when a particular property lingers on the market longer than expected. As a real estate agent, this can be a challenging situation, yet it provides an opportunity to flex your skills and creativity. This section will delve into effective strategies that can help rejuvenate a stale listing and boost its attractiveness to potential buyers.

Price Adjustment
The price tag is often the most critical factor in a property's sale. If a property has been on the market for an extended period, it could be a clear sign that the price is too high compared to similar properties in the area. A thorough Comparative Market Analysis (CMA) can help you determine if a price reduction is necessary to make the property more appealing and competitive. However, remember to communicate this strategy effectively to your sellers, explaining the potential benefits and long-term gains of a price adjustment.

Staging
A well-staged property can significantly increase its attractiveness to potential buyers. If the property has been on the market for a while, it might be worthwhile to invest in professional staging. This could involve rearranging furniture, painting, decluttering, or even bringing in new furniture to enhance the property's appeal. The goal is to help prospective buyers visualize living in the space, making it easier for them to connect emotionally with the property.

High-Quality Photos and Videos
In the digital age, most buyers begin their property search online. Therefore, high-quality photos and videos are instrumental in attracting potential buyers. If a property has been on the market for a long time, consider reshooting the photos or producing a fresh video tour. The new

visuals should highlight the property's best features, including any improvements made since the initial listing.

Marketing Refresh

Revamping your marketing strategy can breathe new life into a stale listing. This could involve targeting a new demographic, boosting your online presence, or utilizing different marketing platforms. Highlight the unique features of the property that make it stand out. Social media, email marketing, and local advertisements can be effective in reaching a wider audience.

Open Houses and Private Showings

An open house can create a buzz around your property and attract a broader audience. Private showings also offer a personalized touch, appealing to serious buyers who appreciate the exclusive viewing opportunity. Both methods provide an intimate experience, allowing potential buyers to inspect the property closely and ask questions directly.

Highlight Community Features

Sometimes, the focus should extend beyond the property itself. Highlighting the neighborhood's desirable features, such as proximity to schools, parks, shopping centers, or public transportation, can enhance the property's appeal. If the property is part of a homeowners association, emphasize any amenities like a community pool, gym, or clubhouse.

Feedback

Lastly, don't overlook the importance of feedback. If potential buyers continually pass on the property, find out why. Their feedback can provide valuable insights into what changes could make the property more appealing.

Patience, persistence, and flexibility are key in selling a property that has been on the market for a while. It might require some trial and error to find the strategy that works best, but with a proactive approach and a willingness to adapt, you can successfully sell any property, regardless of how long it's been on the market.

How would you handle a disagreement with a client over commission rates?

In the world of real estate, commission rates can sometimes become a contentious issue between an agent and a client. Differences may arise over perceptions of worth, value delivered, or the client's financial constraints. However, as a world-class real estate agent, it is crucial to navigate these disagreements professionally, ensuring that both parties' concerns are addressed amicably. This section will guide you through steps to effectively manage a disagreement over commission rates with a client.

It's essential to approach the disagreement with a calm and professional demeanor. Understanding that disagreements are a part of any business relationship will help you maintain your composure. Reacting with emotions can escalate the situation and potentially damage your relationship with the client. Remember, the goal is not to win an argument, but to find a mutually beneficial solution.

Preparation is key. Before any discussion about commission rates, do your homework. Understand the norms in your market, what your competitors charge, and why. Be ready to present this information to your client, explaining why your commission rate is justified based on your skill set, experience, and the value you bring to the transaction. Provide examples of how your expertise has resulted in positive outcomes for previous clients.

Communication is paramount. When a disagreement arises, it's crucial to listen to your client's concerns before presenting your case. Ask open-ended questions to understand their perspective and concerns. Perhaps they are under financial pressure, or maybe they don't fully grasp the amount of work involved in selling or buying a property. By understanding their concerns, you can tailor your response to address these issues specifically.

Transparency and education are vital. Break down what the commission covers, from marketing costs, professional photography, staging, open houses, to your time and expertise in pricing, negotiations, paperwork, and closing the deal. Highlight the value you bring to ensure a smooth, timely transaction and the best possible price. Educating your clients about the intricacies of the work you do can help them understand the justification for your commission rate.

Negotiation is an option. If your client persists in their disagreement about your commission, and you value the relationship or the potential business, you might consider negotiating. This doesn't necessarily mean lowering your rate, but perhaps offering additional services or adjusting payment terms. Remember, your time and expertise are valuable; the aim is to find a balance that satisfies both parties.

Finally, know when to walk away. If, despite your best efforts, the client continues to disagree with your commission rates or undervalue your services, it might be time to part ways. While it's important to be flexible and accommodating, it's equally crucial to stand your ground and protect the value of your work. A professional, respectful exit leaves the door open for future opportunities.

Disagreements over commission rates can be challenging, but they offer an opportunity to demonstrate your professionalism, enhance client understanding, and potentially strengthen the relationship. By approaching these situations with a calm demeanor, thorough preparation, and open communication, you can navigate these disagreements effectively. Remember, your expertise and services as a real estate agent have significant value, and it's essential to protect that value while striving to meet your clients' needs.

13 SPECIAL SITUATIONS

How would you approach selling a historically significant property?

Selling a historically significant property is a unique opportunity for real estate agents. These properties often possess a rich history, architectural significance, and cultural value that sets them apart from conventional listings. Successfully navigating the sale of such properties requires a different approach, as it involves understanding the property's historical context, marketing its unique features, and attracting the right buyer who appreciates its significance. In this question, we will explore the strategies and considerations involved in selling historically significant properties.

Understanding the Historical Context

To effectively sell a historically significant property, it is essential to understand its historical context. Researching the property's history, including its architecture, previous occupants, and any notable events associated with it, allows you to present a compelling narrative to potential buyers. Engage with local historians, preservation societies, and archives to gather valuable information and stories that can be used to create a captivating marketing campaign.

Highlighting Architectural Features

One of the main selling points of historically significant properties is their architectural features. These properties often boast unique designs, craftsmanship, and period-specific details that capture the imagination of potential buyers. Collaborate with architectural experts and preservationists to identify and showcase these features. Professional photography, virtual tours, and 3D renderings can further enhance their visual appeal, enabling buyers to appreciate the property's historical charm.

Leveraging Historical Significance

The historical significance of a property can be a powerful marketing tool. Craft a compelling narrative around the property, emphasizing its historical relevance, and how it contributes to the local community's heritage. This can be done through engaging storytelling in online listings, brochures, and promotional videos. By connecting potential buyers emotionally to the property's past, you increase the chances of attracting those who value historical significance.

Educating Potential Buyers

Selling a historically significant property often requires educating potential buyers about its unique characteristics and potential challenges. Organize guided tours, open houses, or virtual events where interested parties can learn about the property's history, architectural significance, and any preservation restrictions. Educating buyers about the benefits and responsibilities of owning a historically significant property will help them make informed decisions and foster a sense of stewardship.

Networking with Preservation Organizations

To effectively sell a historically significant property, it is essential to network with preservation organizations, local historians, and other experts in the field. These connections can provide valuable insights, resources, and potential buyer referrals. Attend local preservation events, collaborate with historical societies, and engage in conversations with experts to build a strong network that can facilitate the sale of historically significant properties.

Navigating Preservation Restrictions

Historically significant properties may be subject to preservation restrictions or regulations. Familiarize yourself with these guidelines to ensure compliance and inform potential buyers. Understand any limitations or alterations allowed and work closely with preservation organizations, architects, and contractors who specialize in historic renovations. By demonstrating your knowledge of preservation restrictions, you instill confidence in both buyers and sellers, making the purchasing process smoother.

Targeting the Right Market

To sell a historically significant property, it is crucial to identify and target the right market. Marketing efforts should focus on individuals interested in historical properties, preservation enthusiasts, collectors, and those seeking a unique and authentic living experience. Utilize online listing platforms, social media, and targeted advertising to reach this specific audience.

Engage in partnerships with local tourism boards, historical publications, and travel websites to expand your reach and attract potential buyers from outside your immediate area.

Selling a historically significant property requires a specialized approach that goes beyond traditional real estate practices. By understanding the property's historical context, highlighting its architectural features, leveraging its historical significance, and educating potential buyers, you can successfully navigate the sale of these unique properties. Networking with preservation organizations, navigating preservation restrictions, and targeting the right market further enhance your chances of finding the perfect buyer who appreciates and values the historical significance of the property. Embrace the opportunity to contribute to the preservation of our heritage and leave a lasting impact on both the property's legacy and your real estate career.

How would you market a property in a less desirable neighborhood?

In the competitive real estate market, every property has its unique selling points and challenges. As a world-class real estate agent, it is crucial to understand that every neighborhood, even those considered less desirable, offers opportunities for success. In this question, we will discuss effective marketing strategies that can help you sell properties in less desirable neighborhoods, ensuring that you maximize their potential.

Research and Understand the Neighborhood
To effectively market a property in a less desirable neighborhood, you must first thoroughly research and understand the area. This includes studying the local market trends, crime rates, amenities, infrastructure, and any upcoming developments or initiatives that may positively impact the neighborhood. By having this knowledge, you can address potential buyer concerns and highlight the positive aspects of the area during your marketing efforts.

Highlight Unique Selling Points
Every property, regardless of the neighborhood, has unique selling points that can attract potential buyers. Identify and emphasize these aspects when marketing the property. For example, if the property is located near public transportation or has easy access to major highways, emphasize the

convenience of commuting and the potential time savings for buyers. Likewise, if the property has a unique architectural style or features that make it stand out, highlight these attributes to create interest.

Professional Photography and Staging

High-quality photography and staging play an essential role in marketing any property. However, they become even more crucial when marketing a property in a less desirable neighborhood. Professional photographs can showcase the property's best features, making it more appealing to potential buyers. Additionally, staging the property can help potential buyers envision how they could make it their own, regardless of the neighborhood's current condition.

Create an Engaging Online Presence

In today's digital age, an engaging online presence is vital for marketing any property. Develop a comprehensive online marketing strategy that includes using professional photographs, well-written property descriptions, and captivating videos or virtual tours. Utilize popular real estate websites, social media platforms, and your own website to reach potential buyers. By showcasing the property's unique features and benefits, you can generate interest and attract a wider range of potential buyers.

Target Marketing

When marketing a property in a less desirable neighborhood, it is crucial to focus your efforts on the right audience. Identify the buyer demographic that would be most interested in the property and tailor your marketing materials accordingly. For example, if the property is well-suited for first-time homebuyers or investors, create targeted marketing campaigns that highlight the potential return on investment or affordability of the property.

Community Engagement

To overcome the negative perception of a less desirable neighborhood, actively engage with the local community. Attend neighborhood association meetings, volunteer for community events, and establish relationships with local businesses. By demonstrating your commitment to the neighborhood's improvement and showcasing the positive aspects of the community, you can help potential buyers see the neighborhood's potential.

Provide Additional Information

In your marketing materials, provide potential buyers with additional information that addresses any concerns they may have about the neighborhood. This can include statistics on crime reduction initiatives, upcoming development projects, local schools or amenities, and any other positive aspects that can contribute to the neighborhood's desirability. By alleviating buyer concerns, you increase the likelihood of attracting interested parties.

Marketing a property in a less desirable neighborhood requires a strategic approach that highlights its unique selling points and addresses potential buyer concerns. By conducting thorough research, emphasizing the property's best features, utilizing professional photography and staging, creating an engaging online presence, targeting the right audience, engaging with the local community, and providing additional information, you can effectively market and sell properties in less desirable neighborhoods. As a world-class real estate agent, your ability to see the potential in every property and effectively communicate that to potential buyers will set you apart from your competition.

How do you manage transactions involving foreign buyers or sellers?

In today's globalized real estate market, working with foreign buyers or sellers can be a lucrative opportunity for real estate agents. However, it can also present unique challenges and complexities. In this question, we will explore the essential strategies and best practices to successfully manage transactions involving foreign buyers or sellers. From understanding cultural differences to navigating legal and financial considerations, we will equip you with the knowledge and skills necessary to thrive in these international transactions.

Cultural Understanding and Sensitivity
When working with foreign buyers or sellers, cultural understanding and sensitivity are vital for building trust and establishing successful relationships. Recognize that cultural norms, communication styles, and business practices may differ significantly from your own. Take the time to educate yourself about the cultural background of your clients, including their customs, traditions, and etiquette. This will enable you to adapt your approach and tailor your services accordingly. Respect and acknowledge cultural differences to create a positive and inclusive experience for your clients.

Language and Communication

Effective communication is crucial when dealing with foreign buyers or sellers. If you are not fluent in their language, consider hiring a translator or an interpreter to ensure clear and accurate communication throughout the transaction process. Additionally, providing translated marketing materials, contracts, and important documents can help bridge the language barrier and enhance understanding. Stay open-minded, patient, and willing to clarify any misunderstandings that may arise due to language differences.

Legal and Regulatory Considerations

Navigating the legal and regulatory aspects of transactions involving foreign buyers or sellers requires careful attention. Familiarize yourself with the specific laws, regulations, and requirements that pertain to international real estate transactions in your jurisdiction. Seek guidance from legal professionals with expertise in international real estate transactions to ensure compliance and avoid any legal pitfalls. Be aware of any restrictions, taxes, or reporting obligations that may apply to foreign buyers or sellers in your market.

Financing and Currency Exchange

Facilitating financing and managing currency exchange can be intricate when dealing with foreign buyers or sellers. Familiarize yourself with the financing options available to foreign buyers and help them navigate the lending process. Understand the implications of currency exchange rates on the transaction and consult with financial experts to provide guidance to your clients. Collaborate with trusted lenders and currency exchange professionals who have experience in international real estate transactions to ensure a smooth and secure process.

Due Diligence and Documentation

Conducting thorough due diligence and ensuring proper documentation are crucial components of any real estate transaction, particularly when dealing with foreign buyers or sellers. Verify the legitimacy of your clients and their financial capabilities. Familiarize yourself with the necessary documentation required for international transactions, such as passports, identification numbers, and proof of funds. Engage the services of professionals, such as immigration lawyers or accountants, to assist with any immigration or tax-related matters that may arise.

Building a Network

Establishing a strong network of international contacts can greatly benefit your success in managing transactions involving foreign buyers or sellers. Attend international real estate conferences, join industry associations, and participate in networking events to connect with professionals from different countries. Collaborate with local banks, immigration attorneys, and other relevant experts who can provide valuable advice and assistance to your clients. Building relationships with real estate agents in other countries can also enable you to refer clients and expand your global reach.

Successfully managing transactions involving foreign buyers or sellers requires a combination of cultural understanding, effective communication, legal expertise, financial acumen, and due diligence. By investing time and effort into learning about different cultures, staying informed about legal and regulatory requirements, and building a strong network, you can position yourself as a world-class real estate agent capable of thriving in international transactions. Embrace the opportunities that working with foreign buyers or sellers presents, and continuously educate yourself to stay at the forefront of global real estate trends.

How would you handle a property sale in a declining market?

In the unpredictable world of real estate, market fluctuations are inevitable. As a world-class real estate agent, it is crucial to equip yourself with the knowledge and strategies to handle property sales effectively, even in a declining market. While it may seem daunting, a declining market presents unique opportunities for skilled agents to shine and provide invaluable guidance to clients. In this question, we will discuss key tactics and best practices for successfully navigating property sales during a downturn.

Stay Informed and Analyze Market Trends
To effectively handle a property sale in a declining market, it is essential to stay informed and analyze market trends meticulously. Regularly monitor key indicators such as median home prices, average days on the market, and inventory levels. Utilize reliable sources, industry reports, and local market data to gain a comprehensive understanding of the current market conditions. Armed with this knowledge, you can provide clients with accurate information and set realistic expectations.

Price It Right
In a declining market, pricing becomes a critical factor for a successful property sale. Help your clients set an appropriate price by conducting a comprehensive comparative market analysis (CMA). Analyze recently sold properties, current listings, and the specific features and conditions of the client's property. Educate your clients about the importance of pricing

competitively and the potential consequences of overpricing or underpricing. Emphasize the need to attract buyers by offering value within the market's parameters.

Highlight Unique Selling Points

In a declining market, it becomes even more crucial to highlight the unique selling points of a property. Identify and emphasize the features, amenities, and benefits that differentiate the property from others in the market. Showcase any recent renovations, energy-efficient upgrades, or proximity to desirable amenities such as schools, parks, or transportation. Utilize professional photography, virtual tours, and well-crafted marketing materials to present the property in the best possible light.

Strategic Marketing

To maximize exposure and generate interest in a declining market, implement a strategic marketing plan. Leverage both traditional and digital channels to reach a wider audience. Utilize professional staging, photography, and create compelling property descriptions to make a lasting impression. Leverage social media platforms, online listings, and targeted advertising to reach potential buyers. Collaborate with other agents and brokers to expand your network and increase the property's visibility.

Position Yourself as a Trusted Advisor

In a declining market, clients may experience increased anxiety and uncertainty. As their real estate agent, it is your role to position yourself as a trusted advisor and alleviate their concerns. Provide regular updates on market conditions, share relevant data, and offer expert insights to help clients make informed decisions. Demonstrate your knowledge and expertise to instill confidence and build trust. By taking a proactive and empathetic approach, you can guide clients through the process with clarity and professionalism.

Consider Creative Financing Options

During a declining market, financing options may become more restricted, making it essential to explore creative alternatives. Research and suggest financing options such as lease-to-own, seller financing, or rent-to-own arrangements. Collaborate with mortgage brokers and lenders who specialize in challenging market conditions and can offer innovative solutions. By presenting clients with a range of options, you can help them overcome potential hurdles and facilitate a successful sale.

Handling a property sale in a declining market requires adaptability, market knowledge, and strategic thinking. By staying informed, pricing properties competitively, highlighting unique selling points, implementing effective marketing strategies, positioning yourself as a trusted advisor, and considering creative financing options, you can navigate your clients through challenging market conditions. Remember, a world-class real estate agent thrives in any market and uses downturns as opportunities to showcase their expertise and provide exceptional service.

How do you deal with selling properties that have legal issues or liens?

As a real estate agent, you will inevitably come across properties that have legal issues or liens attached to them. These issues can range from minor disputes to complex legal matters, making the process of selling such properties more challenging. However, with proper knowledge and expertise, you can navigate through these obstacles and successfully close deals on properties with legal issues or liens. In this section, we will discuss essential strategies and steps to effectively handle such situations, ensuring a smooth transaction for both the buyer and seller.

Understanding Legal Issues and Liens
Before diving into the strategies for dealing with properties with legal issues or liens, it is crucial to understand what these terms entail. Legal issues can encompass a broad range of complications, including ownership disputes, boundary disputes, zoning violations, or outstanding permits. On the other hand, liens refer to legal claims placed on a property by creditors or government entities due to unpaid debts or obligations. These can include tax liens, mechanics liens, or judgment liens. By being able to identify and understand the specific legal issues or liens affecting a property, you can better advise your clients and take appropriate actions.

Thorough Due Diligence
When encountering a property with legal issues or liens, conducting thorough due diligence is paramount. Begin by reviewing all available property records, including titles, deeds, and any recorded documents related to liens. Engage with experienced real estate attorneys or title companies to ensure a comprehensive examination. Additionally, communicate with the seller to obtain any relevant information about ongoing legal disputes or potential liens. By gathering as much information as possible, you will be better equipped to make informed decisions and

devise a clear strategy.

Educate and Communicate with Clients

Once you have obtained a comprehensive understanding of the legal issues or liens affecting the property, it is essential to educate and communicate with your clients effectively. Explain the implications of these issues, the potential impact on the selling process, and the different options available to proceed. Be transparent about the potential risks involved, ensuring your clients fully comprehend the situation. Establishing open lines of communication built on trust will help manage expectations and reduce any potential conflicts during the transaction.

Engage Professionals

Given the complexities involved in dealing with properties with legal issues or liens, it is crucial to engage professionals who specialize in such matters. This may include real estate attorneys, title companies, or specialized consultants. Collaborating with these experts will provide you and your clients with valuable insights, guidance, and legal protection. They can assist in resolving legal issues, negotiating with creditors, or developing strategies to clear title defects or liens. Remember, a successful real estate agent is one who surrounds themselves with a reliable network of professionals.

Negotiating and Resolving Liens

One of the most critical aspects of selling properties with liens is negotiating with creditors or government entities to resolve these claims. Begin by identifying the type and priority of each lien, as this will affect the order in which they must be addressed. Engage in proactive communication with the lienholders, seeking options for payment plans, lien releases, or settlements. By demonstrating your willingness to work towards a resolution, you can often find viable solutions that satisfy both parties. However, always consult with legal professionals to ensure compliance with local laws and regulations.

Setting Accurate Pricing and Disclosing

When marketing a property with legal issues or liens, it is essential to set the correct pricing and disclose all relevant information to potential buyers. Price the property appropriately, considering the potential costs and efforts required to address the legal issues or liens. Transparency is key, so ensure that all known legal issues are disclosed to potential buyers. This will help attract serious buyers who are willing to navigate through the complexities, reducing the likelihood of surprises or disputes during the closing process.

Dealing with properties that have legal issues or liens can be a challenging task for any real estate agent. However, by implementing the strategies discussed in this section, you can successfully navigate through these obstacles and complete transactions effectively. Remember, thorough due diligence, open communication with clients, collaborating with professionals, and proactive negotiation are the pillars to overcome legal issues or liens. By becoming adept in handling such situations, you can establish yourself as a world-class real estate agent capable of overcoming any obstacle in the industry.

14 COMMERCIAL REAL ESTATE

How does selling commercial property differ from residential property?

In this section, we will explore the nuances of selling commercial property versus residential property. While both branches of the real estate industry offer their own unique challenges and rewards, it is essential for aspiring world-class real estate agents to understand the key differences between the two. By mastering these distinctions, you will be well-equipped to excel in the commercial property market. So, let's dive in.

Market Dynamics
The commercial property market operates on a different scale compared to residential property. Commercial properties are typically larger in size, with multiple units or floors, designed to cater to various businesses. Consequently, the market for commercial properties tends to be more specialized, requiring agents to have a deep understanding of the specific needs and preferences of commercial clients.

Residential properties, on the other hand, cater to individuals or families seeking a place to live. This market is generally more diverse, with varying types of housing, such as apartments, townhouses, and single-family homes. Residential agents must be adept at understanding the unique needs of their clients, including factors like location, amenities, and school districts.

Clientele
When dealing with commercial property, your clients will primarily consist of business owners, investors, and developers. These individuals are typically well-versed in the commercial space and possess a strong understanding of the financial aspects associated with commercial property transactions. Commercial clients often have specific requirements, such as

zoning regulations, lease terms, and potential ROI. As a commercial agent, you must become proficient in analyzing and presenting these complex financial aspects to your clients.

Residential property clients, on the other hand, comprise individuals or families seeking a place to call home. They often rely heavily on their agent's expertise to guide them through the home-buying process. Residential agents must possess exceptional interpersonal skills to understand their clients' desires, budgets, and lifestyle preferences. Building trust and rapport with residential clients is crucial to successfully helping them find their dream home.

Valuation Methods
Valuing commercial properties differs significantly from residential properties. Residential properties are typically evaluated using comparable sales, where recent sales of similar properties in the area are analyzed to determine the market value. This method is widely accepted due to the abundance of residential properties available for comparison.

Commercial properties, on the other hand, require a more comprehensive approach. Valuation methods such as the income approach, cost approach, and sales comparison approach are utilized to determine the property's value. The income approach, which considers the potential rental income, is often the most prevalent method for commercial property valuation. As a commercial agent, understanding these valuation methods and being able to explain them to your clients is vital.

Marketing and Networking
Marketing strategies for commercial and residential properties also differ. Commercial properties often require a more targeted marketing approach, focusing on specific industries or businesses that may benefit from the property's features and location. Networking with professionals such as lawyers, accountants, and business consultants becomes crucial in reaching potential commercial clients.

In contrast, residential properties benefit from a broader marketing approach, targeting a wide range of potential homebuyers. Utilizing online platforms, social media, and hosting open houses are effective ways to attract residential clients. Networking with other residential agents, mortgage brokers, and local community organizations can also expand your reach.

Successfully navigating the commercial property market requires a specialized skill set and a deep understanding of the unique dynamics involved. By recognizing the distinctions between commercial and residential property sales, you will be able to tailor your approach to meet the specific needs of your clients. Remember, whether you choose to specialize in commercial or residential real estate, dedication, ongoing education, and building strong relationships with your clients are key ingredients to becoming a world-class real estate agent.

How do you evaluate the value of a commercial property?

As a world-class real estate agent, one of your key responsibilities is evaluating the value of commercial properties. This crucial skill will enable you to accurately determine the worth of a property, negotiate deals, and provide valuable insights to your clients. In this question, we will delve into the intricacies of evaluating the value of a commercial property. We will explore the various factors that contribute to a property's value and the methodologies used to assess its worth. By mastering these techniques, you will be able to make informed decisions and provide exceptional service to your clients.

Factors Affecting Commercial Property Value
Before delving into the evaluation methods, it is important to understand the key factors that influence the value of a commercial property. These factors can be broadly classified into three categories:

- Location: The old adage "location, location, location" holds true in the commercial real estate industry. The location of a property is a primary determinant of its value. Factors such as proximity to major transportation routes, population density, nearby amenities, and economic growth potential all contribute to the desirability and consequently, the value of a commercial property.
- Physical Attributes: The physical attributes of a property also significantly impact its value. Factors such as lot size, building size, age, condition, architectural design, and the availability of utilities must all be considered. Additionally, features like parking facilities, accessibility, and environmental sustainability measures may also influence a property's value.
- Income Potential: Commercial properties are often viewed as investments, and their income-generating potential plays a vital role in determining their value. Consider the current rental income, lease terms, occupancy rates, and rental growth potential when

138

evaluating a commercial property.

Methods of Property Valuation
To accurately evaluate the value of a commercial property, real estate agents often rely on a combination of methods. Here are three commonly used approaches:

Sales Comparison Approach
The sales comparison approach, also known as the market approach, is a method that involves comparing the subject property to similar properties that have recently been sold. By analyzing recent sales data of comparable properties and making adjustments for differences in size, location, condition, and other relevant factors, you can estimate the value of the subject property. This approach is particularly effective when there is a robust market with sufficient comparable sales data available.

Income Capitalization Approach
The income capitalization approach is primarily used for income-generating commercial properties. It involves estimating the property's value based on its income potential. By calculating the net operating income (NOI) and applying a capitalization rate, which is determined by market trends, you can determine the property's value. This approach is commonly used for properties such as office buildings, retail spaces, and apartment complexes.

Cost Approach
The cost approach determines the value of a property by considering the cost to reproduce or replace it. This method is particularly useful for unique properties or properties with limited sales data. The cost approach involves estimating the land value and the cost of constructing the property, adjusting for depreciation, and adding the value of any improvements. While this approach may not be as commonly used for commercial properties, it is important to understand and consider it when evaluating certain types of properties.

Evaluating the value of a commercial property is a multifaceted process that requires a thorough understanding of the property's location, physical attributes, and income potential. By considering these factors and employing appropriate valuation methods such as the sales comparison approach, income capitalization approach, and cost approach, you will be well-equipped to provide accurate and valuable insights to your clients. Honing your evaluation skills is an ongoing process, and staying updated with market trends and industry knowledge will help you become a world-class real estate agent.

How do you assess a commercial property's potential for return on investment?

As a world-class real estate agent, your ability to assess a commercial property's potential for return on investment (ROI) is crucial. This skill allows you to guide clients towards profitable investments and establish your expertise in the industry. In this question, we will delve into the key factors to consider when evaluating a commercial property's ROI potential, empowering you to make informed decisions and maximize profitability for both yourself and your clients.

Location Analysis

The first and foremost factor to assess is the property's location. Conduct thorough research to understand the local market dynamics, including supply and demand trends, upcoming developments, and economic growth indicators. A property in a prime location with high foot traffic, proximity to popular amenities, and good accessibility will generally yield higher returns on investment compared to properties in less desirable areas.

Market Analysis

Complementing location analysis, evaluating the overall market conditions is vital. Observe both the macro and microeconomic factors affecting the commercial real estate market. Analyze vacancy rates, rental rates, and absorption rates to determine the current state of the market. Additionally, consider the demand and potential growth sectors, such as technology hubs, healthcare facilities, or emerging markets. A healthy and growing market will increase the potential for a successful investment.

Property Condition

The physical condition of the property plays a significant role in assessing its ROI potential. Conduct a thorough inspection to identify any structural, mechanical, or environmental issues that may require immediate or future investments. Additionally, consider the property's age, maintenance history, and compliance with building codes and regulations. A well-maintained property with minimal renovation requirements will yield higher returns compared to one that requires extensive repairs or updates.

Rental Income and Expenses

Analyzing the property's current and potential rental income is crucial in assessing its ROI. Calculate the net operating income (NOI) by subtracting operating expenses, such as property taxes, insurance, utilities, maintenance, and management fees, from the gross rental income. Ensure that the property's rental income is sufficient to cover these expenses while generating a profit. Evaluate lease terms, rental rates, and occupancy rates to estimate future cash flows accurately.

Investment Strategies

Consider different investment strategies that align with the property's potential ROI. Some common strategies include buying and holding for long-term appreciation, value-add opportunities through renovation or repositioning, or lease negotiation for increased rental income. Determine the investment strategy that best suits the property's characteristics, market conditions, and your client's objectives.

Financing Options

Assessing the financing options available for a commercial property is vital when evaluating its ROI potential. Evaluate interest rates, loan terms, and down payment requirements from various lenders. Consider the impact of different financing options on cash flow and overall profitability. Additionally, explore the potential for value appreciation and refinancing options in the future.

Exit Strategy

A sound investment plan includes a well-defined exit strategy. Analyze the potential for capital appreciation, market liquidity, and potential buyers or tenants. Consider the property's long-term potential and the ease of selling or leasing it when the time comes. A well-planned exit strategy ensures a smooth transition and maximizes ROI potential.

Assessing a commercial property's potential for return on investment requires a comprehensive analysis of various factors, including location, market conditions, property condition, rental income, investment strategies, financing options, and exit strategies. By thoroughly evaluating these elements, you can provide valuable insights to your clients, make informed investment decisions, and establish yourself as a world-class real estate agent in the industry. Remember, a deep understanding of these factors will empower you to identify lucrative opportunities, mitigate risks, and ultimately maximize ROI for both yourself and your clients.

How would you market a commercial property to potential investors?

As a world-class real estate agent, one of your primary responsibilities is to effectively market commercial properties to potential investors. The success of this endeavor hinges on your ability to showcase the property's unique features, highlight its investment potential, and capture the attention of the right investors. In this question, we will explore the key strategies and techniques that can help you master the art of marketing commercial properties to potential investors.

Understand the Property

Before you can effectively market a commercial property, it is crucial to thoroughly understand its intricacies. Conduct a comprehensive analysis of the property, including its location, size, zoning regulations, current and potential use, and any existing tenants. Gather all necessary documentation and familiarize yourself with the property's unique selling points.

Develop a Compelling Marketing Strategy:

A successful marketing campaign begins with a well-defined strategy. Start by identifying your target audience – investors who have shown interest in similar properties or have a track record of investing in commercial real estate. Craft a clear message that highlights the property's value proposition, whether it's its potential for high returns, a prime location, or unique features that set it apart from competitors.

Professional Photography and Videos

High-quality visuals play a critical role in attracting potential investors. Hire a professional photographer to capture the property's best angles, emphasizing its unique features. Additionally, consider creating a video tour of the property, showcasing its interior, exterior, and surrounding amenities. Videos can provide a more immersive experience and give potential investors a better sense of the property's potential.

Create a Comprehensive Property Presentation

Compile all relevant information about the commercial property into a comprehensive presentation package. This package should include professional photographs, property details, leasing information, tenant profiles (if applicable), financial projections, and a summary of the property's investment potential. Organize this information in a visually appealing and easily digestible manner, ensuring that the package is both informative and engaging.

Leverage Online Platforms
In today's digital age, online platforms offer unparalleled opportunities to market commercial properties. Utilize listing websites such as LoopNet, CoStar, and Realtor.com to showcase the property to a broad audience of potential investors. Craft an attention-grabbing description that highlights the property's key attributes and investment potential. Additionally, utilize social media platforms, such as LinkedIn, Facebook, and Instagram, to target specific investor demographics and create buzz around the property.

Network with Industry Professionals
Establishing and maintaining relationships with industry professionals can significantly enhance your marketing efforts. Attend real estate conferences, join local real estate associations, and participate in industry events to connect with potential investors. Collaborate with other agents, brokers, and property managers to leverage their networks and tap into their investor databases. By expanding your professional network, you increase the likelihood of finding the right investor for the commercial property.

Develop Customized Marketing Collateral
Tailor your marketing collateral to the specific needs and preferences of potential investors. Create personalized brochures, fact sheets, and presentations that highlight the property's potential return on investment, projected cash flow, lease terms, and other relevant financial information. By customizing your materials, you demonstrate your attention to detail and commitment to meeting the individual investor's requirements.

Host Property Tours and Events
Organize property tours and events to give potential investors the opportunity to experience the property firsthand. Coordinate open houses, networking events, and investor luncheons to create a buzz and generate interest. During these events, highlight the property's key features, answer questions, and engage with potential investors to build relationships and establish trust.

Follow Up and Maintain Communication
After showcasing the property to potential investors, follow up promptly to gauge their level of interest and address any concerns or questions they may have. Maintain ongoing communication to keep investors updated on any developments or changes regarding the property. Building a strong rapport and demonstrating your commitment to transparency and professionalism will enhance the likelihood of closing the deal.

Marketing commercial properties to potential investors requires a strategic approach, a deep understanding of the property's unique features, and the ability to convey its investment potential effectively. By implementing the strategies outlined in this question, you can position yourself as a world-class real estate agent, capable of attracting the right investors and achieving success in the competitive commercial real estate market.

How do you facilitate commercial lease negotiations?

Negotiating commercial leases is a crucial skill for any aspiring world-class real estate agent. The ability to navigate complex negotiations and secure favorable terms for your clients can set you apart as a top-notch professional in the industry. In this question, we will explore the essential steps and strategies required to facilitate successful commercial lease negotiations.

Research and Preparation

Before entering into any negotiation, it is imperative to conduct thorough research and gather relevant information. Start by understanding the local real estate market, including vacancy rates, rental trends, and average lease terms. This knowledge will provide you with a solid foundation to negotiate effectively.

Next, familiarize yourself with the property you are negotiating for. Understand its unique features, strengths, and any potential drawbacks. Analyze the property's historical performance, current tenants, and the landlord's reputation. This information will enable you to identify the property's value proposition and negotiate from a position of strength.

Additionally, research the potential tenant's business and requirements. Understand their industry, growth projections, and specific needs. This knowledge will allow you to align the property's offerings with the tenant's objectives during negotiations.

Define Key Lease Terms

During negotiations, it is vital to clearly define key lease terms to avoid misunderstandings and disputes in the future. Start by determining the lease duration, rent amount, escalation clauses, renewal options, and security deposit requirements. Discuss and document these terms in the letter of intent (LOI) or term sheet, serving as the foundation for the negotiation process.

Establish Open Communication

Establishing open and transparent communication with all parties involved is essential for successful commercial lease negotiations. Regularly engage with the landlord, tenant, and their respective legal representatives to ensure everyone's concerns are heard and addressed. Listen actively to understand their needs, preferences, and pain points, as this will enable you to find mutually beneficial solutions.

Create Win-Win Scenarios

Effective negotiation is not about winning at all costs but rather finding solutions that benefit both parties. Strive for win-win scenarios where both the tenant and landlord feel satisfied with the lease terms. Identify potential areas of compromise and explore creative solutions to address the interests of both parties.

For example, if the tenant requires certain modifications to the space, propose a rent concession in exchange for the landlord covering a portion of the renovation costs. This approach demonstrates your ability to think outside the box and find solutions that meet the needs of both parties.

Anticipate and Address Objections

During commercial lease negotiations, objections are bound to arise. Anticipate potential objections by thoroughly understanding the motivations and concerns of both parties. Be prepared with compelling arguments and data to counter objections effectively. For example, if a tenant objects to the rent increase, provide comparable market data showcasing the property's value and fair market rent.

Leverage Market Conditions

Market conditions can significantly impact the negotiation process. Keep a pulse on the market and leverage favorable conditions to your advantage. For instance, if the market is experiencing high vacancy rates, emphasize the tenant's value and their ability to bring stability to the property. Conversely, in a competitive market, highlight the unique advantages of the property to attract quality tenants.

Facilitating successful commercial lease negotiations requires meticulous research, effective communication, and a strategic approach. By thoroughly preparing, defining key lease terms, fostering open communication, creating win-win scenarios, addressing objections, and leveraging market conditions, you can become a world-class real estate agent capable of securing favorable lease agreements for your clients. Remember, negotiation is an art that can be mastered with practice and experience.

15 LUXURY REAL ESTATE

How does selling luxury real estate differ from typical residential properties?

Congratulations! You have reached a pivotal point in your real estate career – the realm of luxury properties. Selling luxury real estate offers a thrilling and rewarding experience for agents who are ready to elevate their game. However, it is important to note that selling luxury properties differs significantly from the traditional residential market. In this question, we will explore the unique aspects and strategies required to excel in the luxury real estate sector.

Understanding the Luxury Market
Before diving into the intricacies of selling luxury real estate, it is crucial to comprehend the unique dynamics that set this market apart from typical residential properties. The luxury market caters to affluent clients seeking exclusivity, opulence, and an exceptional lifestyle. Therefore, as a world-class real estate agent, your approach must align with the expectations of this distinguished clientele.

Exceptional Properties
Luxury properties are often architectural masterpieces, boasting breathtaking views, exquisite designs, and unparalleled amenities. These homes are the epitome of elegance and are meticulously crafted with the finest materials and finishes. As a luxury real estate agent, you must be adept at showcasing the unique features and the distinct value proposition of each property, emphasizing the exclusivity and prestige it offers.

Niche Market
Unlike the traditional residential market, the luxury sector caters to a niche clientele with specific needs and expectations. Understanding your target

147

audience is key to success in this segment. Luxury buyers are typically discerning individuals who demand personalized attention and exceptional service. Building relationships and maintaining a network within this exclusive community is crucial for securing listings and referrals.

Price Point

The luxury market is characterized by higher price points, often ranging into the millions or even billions. Consequently, the selling process for luxury properties requires a sophisticated approach, meticulous attention to detail, and an in-depth understanding of market trends. Pricing strategies must be carefully formulated, considering the property's unique features, location, and current market conditions.

Navigating the Luxury Market:

Now that we have a solid understanding of the luxury market, let's explore the strategies and techniques necessary to excel in selling luxury real estate.

Expert Knowledge

To establish yourself as a reputable luxury agent, it is imperative to possess comprehensive knowledge of the local luxury market. Stay informed about market trends, upcoming developments, and shifts in demand. Attend industry conferences, network with other luxury agents, and engage in continuous education to expand your expertise. This knowledge will not only impress potential clients but also enable you to offer valuable insights and guidance throughout their buying or selling journey.

Tailored Marketing

Marketing luxury properties requires a more refined and tailored approach. Traditional marketing channels may not suffice in reaching the target luxury clientele. Instead, focus on digital marketing strategies, such as high-quality photography, captivating videos, virtual tours, and well-crafted property descriptions. Utilize social media platforms, targeted online advertising, and establish partnerships with luxury publications to showcase your listings to the right audience.

Discretion and Privacy

Respecting and protecting the privacy of luxury clients is of utmost importance. Luxury buyers and sellers often prefer to keep their transactions confidential. Therefore, as a luxury agent, it is essential to maintain a high level of discretion throughout the entire process. This discretion extends to marketing efforts, ensuring that sensitive information about the property or the client is not disclosed without their explicit permission.

Exceptional Service
Providing exceptional service is the hallmark of a successful luxury real estate agent. Your clients are accustomed to a certain level of service excellence and expect nothing less. Be proactive, responsive, and attentive to their needs. Offer personalized solutions and go above and beyond to deliver a seamless and memorable experience. Building long-lasting relationships based on trust and exceptional service will not only secure your success in the luxury market but also lead to valuable referrals.

Selling luxury real estate is a world of its own, requiring a unique set of skills, knowledge, and strategies. By understanding the distinct dynamics of the luxury market, tailoring your marketing efforts, and providing exceptional service, you can position yourself as a world-class luxury real estate agent. Embrace the challenge, continuously educate yourself, and remember that the rewards of the luxury market are as grand as the properties you will sell.

What special skills are required to be successful in the luxury real estate market?

Essential Skills for Success in the Luxury Real Estate Market
The luxury real estate market is a unique niche within the broader real estate sector. It involves dealing with high-net-worth individuals and properties that are extraordinary in terms of their value, design, location, and amenities. As a real estate agent, thriving in this sector requires a specific skill set that goes beyond the basic competencies of a typical real estate agent. Here are the critical skills necessary to succeed in the luxury real estate market.

1. **Deep Understanding of the Luxury Market:** The luxury real estate market behaves differently from the mainstream market. The factors influencing the purchase decisions of high-net-worth individuals can significantly vary from the average buyer. Agents need to understand these factors and stay updated on market trends, including prices, inventory, buyer preferences, and international influences. This deep understanding is essential to provide valuable insights to clients and to formulate effective sales strategies.

2. **Discretion and Confidentiality:** Privacy is of paramount

importance to many luxury real estate clients. High-profile individuals, including celebrities, executives, and high-net-worth families, often value discretion highly. An agent dealing in this market should be capable of maintaining strict confidentiality and providing a private, secure service.

3. **Exceptional Communication and Negotiation Skills:** Effective communication is key in any real estate transaction, but in the luxury market, it takes on a different dimension. Agents must be articulate, polished, and capable of connecting with their clients on a personal and professional level. Similarly, negotiation skills are crucial. Given the high stakes involved, an effective negotiation can make a considerable difference in the final transaction price.

4. **Personalized Service and Attention to Detail:** Luxury real estate clients often expect a high level of personalized service. They appreciate agents who understand their unique needs, preferences, and lifestyle. A successful luxury real estate agent is meticulous and pays attention to every detail, whether it's staging a property for viewing, crafting a property description, or organizing a seamless transaction process.

5. **Extensive and High-Quality Network:** In the luxury real estate market, who you know often matters as much as what you know. Successful agents have a broad network of contacts, including other agents, high-net-worth individuals, attorneys, and personal advisors. These contacts can often provide leads, referrals, and valuable market information that is not publicly available.

6. **Marketing Prowess:** Luxury properties require a unique marketing approach. High-quality professional photography, virtual tours, and bespoke promotional materials are a must. The ability to effectively utilize digital marketing platforms, including social media, property websites, and email marketing, is also crucial. In some cases, international marketing can be valuable, as the potential buyer may reside in a different country.

7. **Understanding of Luxury Home Features:** Luxury homes often come with features and amenities that are not found in typical homes, such as smart home technology, spa facilities, wine cellars, and more. A luxury real estate agent should be familiar with these features, understand their value, and be able to highlight them effectively to potential buyers.

8. **Patience and Perseverance:** Luxury homes typically take longer to sell due to their high price and a smaller pool of potential buyers. Therefore, patience and perseverance are crucial skills for agents in this market. They should remain proactive and positive, even when a property takes longer to sell.

Succeeding in the luxury real estate market requires a specialized skill set, including deep market knowledge, discretion, effective communication, a high-quality network, personalized service, marketing prowess, a good understanding of luxury features, and patience. By honing these skills, agents can provide an exceptional service to their clients and excel in the luxury real estate market.

How would you market a luxury property to potential buyers?

Marketing luxury properties requires a unique approach compared to marketing other types of real estate. The target audience is affluent individuals who seek exclusivity, sophistication, and unparalleled amenities. In this question, we will explore effective strategies to market luxury properties and attract potential buyers who appreciate the value and exclusivity of such properties.

Understand the target market
To successfully market a luxury property, it is crucial to thoroughly understand the target market. Luxury buyers are often high-net-worth individuals or investors seeking unique and exclusive properties. Conduct market research to identify the demographics, preferences, and lifestyle of potential luxury buyers. Consider their interests, motivations, and online/offline channels they frequent. This understanding will enable you to tailor your marketing strategies accordingly.

Professional Photography and Videography
High-quality visuals are essential when marketing luxury properties. Hiring a professional photographer and videographer is a worthy investment. Capture stunning images that showcase the property's unique features, breathtaking views, and luxurious amenities. Utilize techniques such as aerial photography and virtual tours to provide potential buyers with an immersive experience. These visuals will captivate and entice individuals, leaving a lasting impression.

Utilize Exclusive Listing Platforms
Luxury properties deserve exposure on exclusive listing platforms dedicated to high-end real estate. Online platforms such as LuxuryRealEstate.com, Mansion Global, and Christie's International Real Estate attract affluent buyers actively seeking luxury properties. List your luxury property on these

platforms to increase its visibility among the target market. Leverage the platforms' features, such as extensive property details, high-resolution images, and virtual tours, to showcase the property's unique selling points.

Develop a Compelling Narrative

Luxury buyers are not only purchasing a property; they are investing in a lifestyle. Craft a compelling narrative that highlights the property's unique features, architectural excellence, and the lifestyle it offers. Emphasize exclusivity, privacy, and the exceptional amenities available. Use descriptive language that evokes emotions and paints a vivid picture of the luxury property in the buyer's mind. Incorporate storytelling into your marketing materials, including brochures, listing descriptions, and online content, to engage potential buyers on an emotional level.

Leverage Social Media

Social media platforms offer a vast reach and an opportunity to engage with potential luxury buyers. Utilize platforms such as Instagram, Facebook, LinkedIn, and Twitter to showcase your luxury property. Create visually appealing posts that feature high-quality images, videos, and virtual tours. Engage with your audience by providing insights into the property's unique features, sharing captivating stories, and responding promptly to inquiries. Collaborate with influencers, luxury lifestyle bloggers, and local businesses to extend your reach and attract affluent followers who could be potential buyers.

Host Exclusive Events

Organize exclusive events to showcase the luxury property to potential buyers and real estate professionals within your network. This could include private viewings, cocktail parties, or open houses catered to an upscale audience. Collaborate with luxury brands, interior designers, and architects to provide a complete luxury experience. These events should create a sense of exclusivity and allow potential buyers to envision themselves living the luxury lifestyle offered by the property.

Engage with Local Communities

Engaging with local communities can help foster connections and generate interest in the luxury property. Sponsor local events, charities, or cultural activities that align with the luxury lifestyle. This involvement will not only create a positive brand image but also attract affluent individuals who are active within the community. Collaborate with local media outlets to feature the luxury property in lifestyle magazines, newspapers, or online publications targeted at high-net-worth individuals.

Marketing luxury properties requires a tailored approach that appeals to the desires and expectations of affluent buyers. By understanding the target market, utilizing professional visuals, leveraging exclusive listing platforms, developing a compelling narrative, utilizing social media, hosting exclusive events, and engaging with local communities, you can effectively market luxury properties. Remember, it is crucial to create a captivating and immersive experience that showcases the property's exclusivity, sophistication, and luxurious lifestyle to attract potential buyers and achieve successful sales.

How do you establish connections with high-net-worth individuals?

Establishing connections with high-net-worth individuals (HNWIs) is crucial for any ambitious real estate agent looking to excel in their career. These individuals possess substantial financial resources and often have specific real estate needs or investment goals. By building relationships with HNWIs, you can gain access to exclusive listings, expand your network, and increase your chances of closing lucrative deals. In this question, we will explore effective strategies to establish connections with HNWIs.

Understand the HNWI Landscape
To successfully connect with HNWIs, it is essential to have a clear understanding of their preferences, priorities, and interests. HNWIs are often time-poor and value personalized attention. They expect professionalism, discretion, and expertise from their real estate agents. Educate yourself on the local luxury market, stay updated on emerging trends, and develop a deep knowledge of high-end properties in your area.

Cultivate a Strong Personal Brand
Building a strong personal brand is crucial when connecting with HNWIs. Your brand should reflect professionalism, integrity, and the ability to deliver exceptional service. Craft a compelling personal narrative that showcases your expertise and unique selling points. Establish a strong online presence through a well-designed website, active social media presence, and positive client testimonials. Consistency in your brand message across all platforms will help HNWIs recognize and trust your expertise.

Attend Exclusive Events

HNWIs often attend exclusive events, galas, charity fundraisers, and industry conferences. Research and identify events that attract high-net-worth individuals in your area and make an effort to attend them. These gatherings provide an excellent opportunity to network and build connections with potential clients. Be proactive and engage in meaningful conversations, demonstrating your knowledge of the luxury real estate market without being overly sales-focused.

Leverage Existing Contacts

Your existing network can be a valuable resource when it comes to connecting with HNWIs. Reach out to your past clients, colleagues, friends, and family members who may have connections to high-net-worth individuals. Request introductions or referrals, emphasizing your ability to provide exceptional service to their contacts. Personal recommendations can carry significant weight in the world of HNWIs and may open doors that were previously inaccessible.

Engage with Luxury Service Providers

HNWIs often rely on a network of trusted advisors, including wealth managers, private bankers, attorneys, and accountants. Establish connections with these professionals to increase your chances of meeting HNWIs who require real estate services. Attend industry seminars or events where these individuals gather and offer to educate them about the local luxury real estate market. By positioning yourself as a knowledgeable resource, you can establish trust and potentially receive referrals.

Collaborate with Luxury Brands

Partnering with luxury brands can be a powerful way to connect with HNWIs. Consider forming strategic alliances with high-end car dealerships, luxury fashion boutiques, or high-profile interior designers. Explore opportunities for cross-promotion, joint events, or co-branded marketing initiatives. By associating yourself with reputable luxury brands, you can enhance your credibility and attract the attention of HNWIs who value these brands.

Provide Value and Expertise

To establish connections with HNWIs, it is essential to provide value and demonstrate your expertise in the luxury real estate market. Publish informative articles or blog posts on topics relevant to HNWIs, such as investment strategies, property trends, or tax implications of real estate transactions. Consider hosting exclusive educational events for HNWIs, offering insights into the local market or investment opportunities. By positioning yourself as a trusted advisor, you can build lasting connections with HNWIs who appreciate your knowledge and guidance.

Connecting with high-net-worth individuals is an art that requires a combination of industry knowledge, personal branding, networking skills, and providing exceptional service. By understanding their preferences, attending exclusive events, leveraging existing contacts, collaborating with luxury brands, and demonstrating expertise, you can establish meaningful connections with HNWIs and position yourself as a world-class real estate agent. Remember, building relationships takes time, persistence, and genuine effort. Stay committed to nurturing these connections, and the rewards will follow.

How do you manage confidentiality and discretion in luxury transactions?

In the world of real estate, confidentiality and discretion are crucial elements for success, especially when dealing with luxury transactions. As a world-class real estate agent, you must understand and prioritize the importance of maintaining the trust and privacy of your high-profile clients. This section will guide you through various strategies and best practices for managing confidentiality and discretion in luxury transactions, ensuring the utmost professionalism and integrity in your real estate career.

Establishing Trust and Confidentiality
Building trust with your clients is the foundation for maintaining confidentiality and discretion. From the very first interaction, make it clear that you prioritize their privacy and understand the sensitivity of luxury transactions. Assure them that their personal information and details regarding the transaction will be handled with the utmost care and confidentiality.

Non-Disclosure Agreements (NDAs)
In luxury transactions, it is often prudent to consider implementing non-disclosure agreements (NDAs) to protect your clients' sensitive information. An NDA is a legally binding document that prohibits the disclosure of confidential information to any third party without the client's explicit consent. By having your clients sign an NDA, you demonstrate your commitment to maintaining confidentiality, and it provides an extra layer of protection for your clients and the transaction.

Limiting Access to Information

Ensure that access to sensitive information is limited only to individuals who absolutely need it. Restricting access helps minimize the risk of unintentional disclosures. Share information on a need-to-know basis with your team members, colleagues, and other professionals involved in the transaction. Emphasize the importance of confidentiality to everyone involved and maintain a culture of discretion within your team.

Secure Communication Channels

Luxury transactions often involve exchanging sensitive information, such as financial details, legal documents, and personal preferences. To maintain confidentiality, it is crucial to use secure communication channels when sharing such information. Encourage the use of secure email platforms, encrypted messaging apps, and virtual data rooms to ensure the privacy of your clients' information.

Professionalism and Discretion

Always conduct yourself with the utmost professionalism and discretion, both in-person and online. Be mindful of what you share on social media platforms, as even seemingly innocent posts can inadvertently reveal information about your high-profile clients or luxury transactions. Maintain a strict code of conduct and avoid discussing client matters outside of professional settings.

Collaborating with Trusted Professionals

In luxury transactions, you may often work alongside various professionals, such as attorneys, accountants, and other real estate agents. It is essential to collaborate with trusted professionals who understand the importance of confidentiality and discretion. Vet each professional you work with, ensuring they have a track record of professionalism and respect for client privacy.

Managing Open Houses and Showings

When dealing with luxury properties, managing confidentiality during open houses and showings becomes even more critical. Consider implementing controlled access measures, such as pre-screening potential buyers and requiring them to sign NDAs before attending exclusive showings. Limit the number of people present during showings and instruct your team to discreetly monitor and ensure the privacy of your clients' properties.

Respect for Privacy

Respect your clients' privacy at all times. Never disclose their names or any personal information without their explicit consent. Be cautious when discussing their transactions or properties with colleagues or friends, even in casual conversations. Always prioritize their privacy and maintain the confidentiality of their information long after the transaction concludes.

Managing confidentiality and discretion in luxury transactions is an essential characteristic of a world-class real estate agent. By establishing trust, implementing NDAs, limiting access to information, using secure communication channels, maintaining professionalism, collaborating with trusted professionals, and respecting privacy, you can ensure your high-profile clients' confidentiality and protect their interests throughout the luxury transaction process. Confidentiality is not just a professional obligation; it is a cornerstone of your reputation and success as an exceptional real estate agent.

16 REAL ESTATE INVESTING

How do you evaluate a property for its investment potential?

As a real estate agent, it is crucial to possess the ability to evaluate properties for their investment potential. This skill will not only help you provide valuable insights to your clients but also allow you to make informed decisions for your own real estate ventures. In this question, we will delve into the various factors to consider when evaluating a property's investment potential, empowering you to become a world-class real estate agent.

Location Analysis
One of the most significant factors influencing a property's investment potential is its location. Consider the following aspects when evaluating a property:

a) Neighborhood: Research the area's demographics, crime rates, school district ratings, proximity to amenities, and employment opportunities. A favorable neighborhood will attract tenants or buyers and ensure a steady demand for the property.

b) Economic Growth: Examine the local economy's stability, job market, and potential for growth. Areas experiencing economic expansion tend to yield better returns on investment.

c) Transportation and Accessibility: Evaluate the property's access to public transportation, major highways, airports, and proximity to urban centers. Properties with convenient transportation options are often more desirable.

Property Condition and Maintenance
Assessing the property's condition is essential to determine its investment

potential. Consider the following factors:

a) Physical Condition: Conduct a thorough inspection of the property, including its structural integrity, foundation, roof, plumbing, electrical systems, heating, ventilation, and air conditioning (HVAC). Any major repairs or renovations required can significantly impact the investment potential.

b) Maintenance Requirements: Evaluate the property's ongoing maintenance needs, such as landscaping, exterior repairs, and common area upkeep for multifamily properties. High maintenance costs can eat into potential returns.

Market Analysis
Understanding the real estate market is crucial when evaluating a property's investment potential. Consider the following key market indicators:

a) Supply and Demand: Study the current market trends to gauge the supply and demand dynamics. A high demand and limited supply can lead to increased property values and rental rates.

b) Comparable Sales and Rental Rates: Analyze recent sales and rental data for similar properties in the area. This information will help you determine if the property is priced competitively and whether it aligns with the expected returns.

c) Market Appreciation: Research the historical and projected market appreciation rates. Areas with consistent appreciation tend to be more favorable for long-term investments.

Financial Analysis
To evaluate the investment potential of a property accurately, you must conduct a comprehensive financial analysis. Consider the following aspects:

a) Cash Flow: Calculate the property's potential cash flow by subtracting all expenses (mortgage payments, property taxes, insurance, maintenance costs, etc.) from the expected rental income. A positive cash flow indicates a potentially lucrative investment.

b) Return on Investment (ROI): Determine the projected ROI by comparing the property's expected annual income to the initial investment. This will help you assess the property's profitability and compare it to other investment opportunities.

c) Financing Options: Explore different financing options available for the property, such as traditional mortgages, private lenders, or partnerships. Understand the terms, interest rates, and potential risks associated with each option.

Risk Assessment
Lastly, it is crucial to evaluate and mitigate potential risks associated with the property. Consider the following risk factors:

a) Market Risk: Analyze the market's stability and the potential impact of economic fluctuations on property values and rental rates.

b) Tenant Risk: Assess the potential tenant pool and associated risks, such as vacancy rates, tenant turnover, and potential default on rental payments.

c) Legal and Regulatory Factors: Understand local laws, regulations, and zoning restrictions that may impact the property's use, rental restrictions, or future development plans.

Evaluating a property's investment potential requires a comprehensive analysis of various factors such as location, property condition, market analysis, financial considerations, and risk assessment. By honing your expertise in these areas, you will become a world-class real estate agent capable of guiding clients towards profitable investments and making wise decisions for your own portfolio. Remember, thorough evaluation is the key to unlocking the hidden potential of any property.

How do you guide a client in building a real estate investment portfolio?

As a world-class real estate agent, it is not only your responsibility to help clients find their dream homes but also to guide them in building a real estate investment portfolio. A well-diversified portfolio can provide a steady income stream, long-term wealth accumulation, and financial security. In this question, we will explore the essential steps and strategies to effectively guide clients in building a robust real estate investment portfolio.

Determine the Client's Investment Goals and Risk Tolerance
Before embarking on the journey of building a real estate investment

portfolio, it is crucial to have a clear understanding of your client's investment goals and risk tolerance. Some clients may seek immediate cash flow, while others may have a long-term appreciation strategy. Similarly, risk tolerance can vary from conservative to aggressive. By identifying these factors, you can tailor your guidance and recommendations accordingly.

Educate Clients about Different Investment Strategies
Real estate offers numerous investment strategies, each with its own benefits and risks. It is imperative to educate your clients about these strategies to help them make informed decisions. Discuss strategies like rental properties, fix-and-flip, vacation rentals, commercial properties, or real estate investment trusts (REITs). Explain the pros and cons of each strategy, emphasizing factors such as cash flow potential, market conditions, and property management requirements.

Analyze Market Conditions and Conduct Thorough Research
To guide clients effectively, it is essential to stay up-to-date with market trends, economic indicators, and local real estate conditions. Conduct thorough research and analysis to identify emerging areas, potential investment hotspots, and market drivers. Provide your clients with comprehensive data on market appreciation rates, vacancy rates, rental yields, and any legal or regulatory considerations that may impact their investment decisions.

Help Clients Identify Suitable Properties
Once you have a comprehensive understanding of your client's investment goals and market conditions, assist them in identifying suitable properties. Consider factors like location, property type, condition, potential rental income, and growth potential. Help your clients conduct due diligence, including property inspections, title searches, and financial analysis. Encourage them to envision the property's long-term potential and how it aligns with their investment goals.

Financial Planning and Financing Options
Building a real estate investment portfolio requires careful financial planning. Collaborate with your client's financial advisor or recommend trustworthy professionals who can assist in creating a solid financial plan. Explore various financing options, such as traditional mortgages, seller financing, or partnerships. Educate your clients about the impact of interest rates, loan terms, and down payments on their cash flow and return on investment.

Property Management and Maintenance

An often overlooked aspect of building a real estate investment portfolio is property management. Highlight the significance of efficient property management for maximizing returns and minimizing headaches. Educate your clients about self-management versus hiring professional property management companies. Discuss the responsibilities of property owners, legal obligations, and the importance of maintenance and repairs to preserve property value.

Monitor and Adjust the Portfolio

Building a real estate investment portfolio is an ongoing process. Advise your clients to regularly monitor their investments, track cash flow, and evaluate property performance. Encourage them to stay informed about market changes and reassess their investment strategy periodically. Help them identify opportunities to diversify their portfolio, acquire additional properties, or sell underperforming assets.

Guiding clients in building a real estate investment portfolio requires a comprehensive understanding of their goals, market conditions, and investment strategies. By following the steps outlined in this question, you can provide valuable guidance to your clients, helping them create a robust and profitable real estate investment portfolio. Building a successful portfolio is a long-term endeavor that requires continuous learning, adaptation, and diligent monitoring.

How do you manage properties for real estate investors?

Managing properties for real estate investors is a crucial aspect of being a world-class real estate agent. As an agent, you must not only excel in finding profitable investment opportunities but also possess the skills to effectively oversee and manage these properties on behalf of your clients. In this question, we will explore the key principles and strategies involved in managing properties for real estate investors.

Understanding the Investor's Goals

Before diving into property management, it is essential to understand the goals and objectives of the real estate investor. Whether the investor is seeking long-term cash flow, property appreciation, or a combination of both, their objectives will shape your management strategy. By aligning your management approach with the investor's goals, you can build a successful and profitable partnership.

Establishing Effective Communication
Effective communication is the foundation of successful property management. From the beginning, establish clear lines of communication with your clients. Regularly update them on property performance, potential issues, and any necessary actions. Additionally, ensure that you are readily available to address any concerns or questions they may have. By maintaining open and transparent communication, you can build trust and foster a strong working relationship with your clients.

Tenant Screening and Selection
One of the critical responsibilities of managing properties is tenant screening and selection. It is essential to find reliable and responsible tenants who will pay rent on time and maintain the property. Develop a thorough screening process that includes background checks, credit history, employment verification, and references. By selecting high-quality tenants, you can minimize potential issues and ensure a smooth rental experience.

Lease Agreements and Compliance
Creating comprehensive lease agreements is paramount to protecting both the investor's interests and the tenants' rights. Ensure that lease agreements outline the terms of the tenancy, including rental amount, due dates, security deposit details, maintenance responsibilities, and any specific rules or regulations. Familiarize yourself with local and federal laws governing rental properties to ensure compliance and avoid legal issues.

Rent Collection and Financial Management
Efficient rent collection is crucial for maintaining positive cash flow. Establish clear rent collection procedures and enforce them consistently. Utilize technology to streamline the process, offering online payment options to tenants. Additionally, stay on top of financial management, including tracking income and expenses, budgeting for property maintenance and repairs, and providing regular financial reports to investors.

Property Maintenance and Repairs
Proactive property maintenance is crucial for preserving the value of the investment and ensuring tenant satisfaction. Regularly inspect properties to identify any maintenance or repair needs promptly. Develop a network of reliable contractors and vendors to address these issues efficiently. By promptly addressing maintenance requests and maintaining the property's condition, you can minimize vacancy periods and increase tenant retention.

Handling Tenant Relations

Managing tenant relations is an ongoing responsibility. It is essential to promptly address tenant concerns, requests, and complaints. Foster a positive tenant experience by being responsive, respectful, and fair. Encourage open communication and provide a clear process for reporting issues or requesting repairs. By establishing a supportive and respectful relationship with tenants, you can enhance tenant satisfaction and reduce turnover.

Property Inspections and Evaluations

Regular property inspections and evaluations are crucial for identifying potential issues and ensuring compliance with lease agreements. Conduct routine inspections to assess the property's condition, identify any necessary repairs or maintenance, and ensure tenants are adhering to the lease terms. Communicate inspection results to both the investor and the tenants to maintain transparency and address any necessary actions promptly.

Managing properties for real estate investors requires a comprehensive approach that balances the investor's objectives, tenant satisfaction, and property maintenance. By effectively communicating with your clients, implementing rigorous tenant screening processes, complying with legal requirements, and prioritizing property maintenance, you can establish yourself as a world-class real estate agent. Successful property management is not only about maximizing returns but also about building strong and lasting relationships with both investors and tenants.

How do you analyze the risk and return of real estate investments?

As a world-class real estate agent, it is imperative to have a deep understanding of how to analyze the risk and return of real estate investments. Evaluating these factors allows you to make informed decisions, select the most profitable opportunities, and provide valuable advice to your clients. In this question, we will delve into the key components and methodologies to effectively analyze the risk and return of real estate investments.

Assessing Risk

Risk assessment is crucial in real estate investment analysis as it helps you understand the potential downsides and uncertainties associated with a particular property or investment opportunity. Here are some key steps to consider:

a.) Market Analysis: Begin by researching and analyzing the local real estate market to identify trends, demand, and supply dynamics. Factors such as population growth, job opportunities, infrastructure development, and economic stability affect market risk.

b.) Property-Specific Analysis: Evaluate the property's location, condition, zoning regulations, and potential for future growth. Consider factors such as proximity to amenities, schools, transportation, and crime rates. Assessing these aspects helps determine the inherent risk associated with the property.

c.) Financial Analysis: Conduct a thorough financial analysis to estimate the investment's potential returns, cash flows, and profitability. This includes assessing rental income, property expenses, financing costs, and potential tax implications. Analyzing the financial aspects helps gauge the risk associated with the investment.

d.) Risk Diversification: Diversifying your real estate portfolio across property types, locations, and investment strategies can help mitigate risk. By spreading your investments, you reduce the potential negative impact of a single investment on your overall portfolio.

Quantifying Return
Understanding the potential return on investment (ROI) is equally important when analyzing real estate investments. Here are some key considerations:

a.) Cash Flow Analysis: Evaluate the property's cash flow potential by estimating rental income, deducting expenses (e.g., property taxes, insurance, maintenance), and factoring in financing costs. Positive cash flow indicates a potentially attractive investment.

b.) Appreciation Potential: Assess the property's appreciation potential by analyzing historical price trends and market forecasts. Properties in areas with strong economic growth and high demand tend to appreciate more. However, it's important to remember that appreciation is speculative and subject to market fluctuations.

c.) Equity Build-Up: Consider the property's potential for equity build-up through loan amortization. As you pay down the mortgage, your equity in the property increases, providing long-term wealth accumulation opportunities.

d.) Tax Benefits: Analyze the tax advantages associated with real estate investments, such as deductions for mortgage interest, property taxes, and depreciation. These benefits can positively impact your returns and overall profitability.

Risk-Return Tradeoff

Analyzing the risk-return tradeoff is essential when evaluating real estate investments. Typically, higher returns are associated with higher risks. It is crucial to strike a balance between risk and potential reward based on your risk appetite and investment goals.

a.) Risk Assessment Matrix: Develop a risk assessment matrix to categorize various investment opportunities based on their risk and return profiles. This matrix will help you compare and prioritize investments.

b.) Return on Investment (ROI): Calculate the ROI for each investment opportunity by considering the expected cash flows, appreciation potential, and equity build-up over the investment period. This allows for a standardized comparison of returns across different investments.

c.) Sensitivity Analysis: Perform sensitivity analysis by testing the potential impact of different market scenarios on investment returns. This helps you understand the investment's resilience to market fluctuations and unforeseen events.

Analyzing the risk and return of real estate investments is a critical skill for a world-class real estate agent. By assessing the risks associated with a property, quantifying potential returns, and understanding the risk-return tradeoff, you can make informed investment decisions and provide valuable guidance to your clients. Remember, thorough analysis and a balanced approach are key to becoming a successful real estate investor.

How do you handle real estate transactions involving Real Estate Investment Trusts (REITs)?

Real Estate Investment Trusts (REITs) have become a significant player in the real estate industry, offering investors an opportunity to participate in large-scale real estate projects without the burden of direct ownership. As a world-class real estate agent, it is crucial to understand the intricacies of working with REITs and effectively navigate transactions involving these entities. In this question, we will explore the fundamentals of handling real estate transactions involving REITs, including identifying potential opportunities, building relationships, and executing successful deals.

Understanding REITs

Before delving into the specifics of handling transactions involving REITs, it is essential to have a solid understanding of what REITs are and how they operate. A REIT is a company that owns, operates, or finances income-generating real estate. They pool funds from various investors to invest in a diverse portfolio of properties, such as commercial buildings, apartment complexes, or shopping centers. REITs are required by law to distribute a significant portion of their income to shareholders, making them an attractive investment for those seeking consistent cash flow.

Identifying and Evaluating Opportunities

When it comes to working with REITs, identifying potential opportunities starts with thorough market research. Stay updated on local and national real estate trends, including areas experiencing growth and those with high demand for specific property types. Analyze market reports, attend industry conferences, and network with professionals in the field to gain valuable insights into potential investment opportunities that REITs might be interested in pursuing.

Once you have identified potential opportunities, it is crucial to evaluate them from the perspective of a REIT. REITs often have specific investment criteria, such as property type, location, and return on investment expectations. Understand these criteria and tailor your proposal accordingly. Conduct a thorough analysis of the property, including its financial performance, potential for growth, and any legal or environmental considerations. Presenting a well-researched opportunity that aligns with a REIT's investment goals will significantly increase your chances of success.

Building Relationships with REITs

Establishing strong relationships with REITs is key to becoming a go-to real estate agent in this niche. Attend industry events where REIT representatives are likely to be present and make an effort to connect with them personally. Be proactive in reaching out to REITs through phone calls, emails, or arranging face-to-face meetings to discuss potential collaboration opportunities. Building trust and rapport with REITs takes time, so be patient and persistent in your efforts.

During your interactions with REITs, it is vital to showcase your expertise and knowledge of the real estate market. Provide them with comprehensive market reports, analysis of potential investment opportunities, and insights into emerging trends. By positioning yourself as a valuable resource, you will increase your chances of being considered for future transactions.

Executing Successful Deals

Once you have established a relationship with a REIT and identified a mutually beneficial opportunity, it is time to execute the transaction. The process of handling transactions involving REITs is similar to traditional real estate deals but with some additional considerations.

Due Diligence: Conduct thorough due diligence to ensure all legal, financial, and operational aspects of the property are in order. This includes reviewing leases, financial statements, environmental reports, and any other relevant documentation.

Negotiations

Negotiate the terms of the transaction, keeping in mind the specific requirements and investment goals of the REIT. Be prepared to negotiate on price, terms, and any contingencies that may arise during the process.

Documentation: Prepare all necessary legal documents, including purchase agreements, financing agreements, and any additional agreements specific to the REIT's requirements. It is advisable to involve a qualified real estate attorney to ensure compliance and protect your client's interests.

Communication and Coordination: Throughout the transaction, maintain open lines of communication with all parties involved, including the REIT, sellers, lenders, and attorneys. Ensure that everyone is on the same page and that deadlines are met promptly.

Closing and Post-Closing

Facilitate a smooth closing process, ensuring all necessary documentation and funds are in place. Following the closing, maintain contact with the REIT to address any post-closing matters and solidify your relationship for future opportunities.

Handling real estate transactions involving REITs requires a thorough understanding of these specialized investment entities and the ability to identify, evaluate, and execute lucrative opportunities. By building strong relationships with REITs, showcasing your expertise, and diligently managing the transaction process, you can become a trusted advisor in the world of real estate investments. Stay up-to-date with market trends, continue expanding your network, and always strive for excellence in providing top-notch service to both REITs and their investors.

17 REAL ESTATE LAW AND REGULATIONS

How do I protect myself from legal liability as a real estate agent?

As a real estate agent, it is crucial to understand and mitigate potential legal risks associated with your profession. A proactive approach to protect yourself from legal liability not only safeguards your interests but also builds trust with clients and enhances your professional reputation. This section will outline key steps and practices you can adopt to minimize legal risks and ensure a successful and ethical real estate career.

Obtain Proper Licensing and Education
To operate as a real estate agent, it is essential to obtain the appropriate licensing and complete the necessary education requirements mandated by your jurisdiction. Complying with these legal prerequisites enables you to conduct business legally and demonstrates your commitment to professionalism and industry standards.

Maintain Knowledge and Stay Updated
Real estate laws and regulations are subject to change, and it is essential to stay informed about any updates relevant to your practice. Regularly attending professional development courses, seminars, and workshops will help you stay up-to-date on legal requirements, contracts, disclosure obligations, fair housing laws, and other legal aspects of the industry. Being well-informed not only protects you but also allows you to better serve your clients.

Work with a Qualified Brokerage
Choosing a reputable and experienced brokerage to work with is vital. A good brokerage will provide guidance, support, and supervision, helping to minimize legal risks. Ensure the brokerage has a solid reputation, maintains

proper insurance coverage, and has established risk management protocols in place. Collaborating with an established brokerage can offer you access to legal resources, advice, and mentorship.

Use Clear and Detailed Contracts

Contracts are the foundation of any real estate transaction, and it is crucial to draft clear, detailed, and legally sound agreements that protect all parties involved. Consult with legal professionals or use standardized contract forms provided by your local real estate association or regulatory body. Avoid using vague or ambiguous language and ensure all parties fully understand and agree to the terms outlined in the contract.

Practice Full Disclosure

Honesty and transparency are vital in real estate transactions. Disclose all material facts, known defects, and potential issues related to a property, even if it means potential setbacks or loss of a sale. Failure to disclose can lead to legal consequences, loss of reputation, and damage to client relationships. Maintaining detailed records of all disclosures will provide evidence of your compliance with disclosure obligations.

Maintain Accurate and Organized Records

Keeping thorough and organized records of all transactions, communications, and client interactions is essential. Accurate records serve as evidence in case of disputes or legal proceedings. Maintain copies of contracts, agreements, and any correspondence related to transactions. Additionally, ensure you comply with data protection laws and maintain client confidentiality.

Obtain Appropriate Insurance Coverage

Real estate professionals face various risks, including claims of negligence, errors, omissions, or even discrimination. It is crucial to obtain appropriate professional liability insurance coverage to safeguard against potential legal claims. Consult with insurance professionals specializing in real estate to assess your specific needs and obtain adequate coverage.

Communicate Clearly and Manage Expectations

Effective communication is key to avoiding misunderstandings and potential legal disputes. Clearly communicate all terms, conditions, and expectations to clients, ensuring they understand the implications of any decisions made. Document all discussions and agreements in writing to avoid any misinterpretation or later disputes.

Protecting yourself from legal liability as a real estate agent requires a proactive and diligent approach. By obtaining proper licensing, staying educated and informed, working with a reputable brokerage, using clear contracts, practicing full disclosure, maintaining accurate records, obtaining insurance coverage, and practicing effective communication, you lay a strong foundation for a successful and legally compliant real estate career. Always consult with legal professionals for advice tailored to your specific jurisdiction and circumstances to ensure you have the necessary protection in place.

How well do you understand real estate laws and regulations?

To become a world-class real estate agent, it is crucial to have a deep understanding of real estate laws and regulations. These laws govern every aspect of the industry, from property transactions to contracts, disclosures, and advertising practices. Failing to grasp these laws and regulations can lead to legal complications, potential lawsuits, and damage to your reputation. In this question, we will explore the importance of understanding real estate laws and regulations, the key areas you need to be well-versed in, and ways to ensure compliance.

The Significance of Real Estate Laws and Regulations
Real estate laws and regulations exist to protect the rights and interests of all parties involved in real estate transactions. As a real estate agent, it is your responsibility to guide clients through the complex legal landscape, ensuring their best interests are safeguarded. By having a solid understanding of these laws, you can provide accurate information, minimize risks, and build trust with your clients.

Key Areas of Real Estate Laws and Regulations
Property Transactions: Real estate laws govern the purchase, sale, and transfer of properties. It is essential to understand the legal requirements for drafting and executing contracts, conducting property inspections, negotiating offers, and ensuring clear title ownership. Familiarize yourself with the laws governing purchase agreements, contingencies, financing, and closing procedures to facilitate smooth and legally compliant transactions.

Disclosures and Representations: As a real estate agent, you have a legal obligation to disclose all material facts about a property to potential buyers. Failure to disclose could lead to lawsuits and financial consequences.

Educate yourself on the laws and regulations surrounding disclosure of property defects, lead-based paint, environmental hazards, and any other relevant information that might affect the buyer's decision-making process.

Fair Housing Laws: Fair housing laws aim to prevent discrimination in the sale, rental, and financing of properties. Familiarize yourself with federal, state, and local fair housing laws, which prohibit discrimination based on race, color, religion, sex, national origin, familial status, and disability. Understand the rules related to advertising, showing properties, and ensuring equal treatment for all clients.

Landlord-Tenant Laws: If you handle rental properties, understanding landlord-tenant laws is crucial. These laws dictate the rights and responsibilities of both landlords and tenants. Familiarize yourself with regulations concerning lease agreements, security deposits, eviction processes, habitability standards, and rent control laws, among other relevant topics.

Advertising and Marketing: Real estate agents must adhere to strict regulations when it comes to advertising and marketing properties. Understand the guidelines surrounding truthful and non-deceptive advertising, avoiding discriminatory language, and ensuring compliance with local advertising regulations. Stay updated on digital advertising practices, as online platforms have specific rules for real estate agents.

Ensuring Compliance: To ensure compliance with real estate laws and regulations, consider the following strategies:

Continuous Education: Stay informed about changes and updates in real estate laws through ongoing education. Attend seminars, webinars, and workshops to enhance your knowledge and understanding of the legal landscape. Many professional organizations offer courses specifically focused on real estate laws and regulations.

Consult Legal Professionals: When in doubt or faced with complex legal situations, consult with a real estate attorney. They can provide guidance, review contracts, and help you navigate legal challenges. Developing a professional relationship with a reputable attorney can be invaluable throughout your real estate career.

Partner with a Brokerage: Joining a reputable brokerage with a strong legal support system can provide you with access to legal expertise and resources. Many brokerages have legal departments or retain legal counsel to assist their agents when needed. This collaboration ensures you have the necessary support to navigate legal complexities.

Stay Up to Date
Real estate laws and regulations evolve over time. Make it a habit to stay updated with changes in legislation at the local, state, and federal levels. Subscribe to industry newsletters, follow reliable legal resources, and join professional associations to receive timely updates about any legal amendments.

Mastering real estate laws and regulations is a fundamental aspect of becoming a world-class real estate agent. By understanding the legal landscape, you can protect your clients, mitigate risks, and conduct business ethically and responsibly. Embrace continuous learning, consult legal professionals when needed, and stay updated to ensure compliance with the ever-evolving legal framework of the real estate industry.

How do you ensure compliance with fair housing laws in your profession?

As a world-class real estate agent, maintaining the highest standards of professionalism and ethics is crucial to your success. One of the fundamental pillars of real estate practice is ensuring compliance with fair housing laws. These laws provide equal opportunity and protect against discrimination in housing transactions. By understanding and adhering to fair housing laws, you not only fulfill your legal obligations but also foster trust and credibility with clients and colleagues alike. In this section, we will explore the key principles and practical steps you can take to ensure compliance with fair housing laws in your profession.

Understanding Fair Housing Laws
Fair housing laws have been enacted to eliminate discrimination based on race, color, religion, national origin, sex, familial status, and disability. Familiarize yourself with the fair housing laws applicable in your jurisdiction, such as the Fair Housing Act in the United States, and stay updated on any amendments or additions. Additionally, become knowledgeable about any local, state, or federal fair housing agencies or organizations that provide resources and support to real estate professionals.

Adopting a Non-Discriminatory Mindset

Creating an inclusive and fair housing environment starts with your mindset. Embrace diversity and treat all clients with equal respect and consideration, regardless of their background or personal characteristics. Avoid making assumptions or stereotypes based on protected classes, and focus on providing exceptional service to all clients. Remember, fair housing laws are not just legal requirements but ethical imperatives that underpin the integrity of your profession.

Practical Steps to Ensure Compliance

Educate Yourself and Your Team: Stay informed about fair housing laws by attending training sessions, workshops, or webinars offered by reputable organizations. Encourage your team members to do the same and provide resources, such as educational materials or online courses, to facilitate their understanding of fair housing principles and best practices. Regularly discuss fair housing topics during team meetings to reinforce their importance.

Develop Clear Policies and Procedures: Create a written fair housing policy for your agency that outlines your commitment to compliance and non-discrimination. Clearly communicate this policy to all employees, agents, and partners, and ensure they understand its implications. Establish procedures for handling inquiries, showings, and negotiations that prioritize fair treatment and equal opportunity for all clients.

Provide Equal Access to Information: Make sure that all clients have equal access to information about available properties, including listings, brochures, and online resources. Avoid steering clients towards or away from certain areas or properties based on protected characteristics. Present properties neutrally and focus on their features, amenities, and suitability for clients' needs.

Implement Unbiased Advertising and Marketing Strategies: Review your advertising and marketing materials to ensure they comply with fair housing principles. Avoid using language, images, or symbols that might imply a preference or exclusion based on protected classes. Use inclusive and diverse imagery that reflects the communities you serve. When describing properties, focus on objective details rather than potentially discriminatory factors.

Treat All Clients Equally: When working with potential buyers or tenants, provide the same level of service and attention to all individuals. Avoid making assumptions or judgments about their preferences or suitability for certain properties. Ensure equal treatment during property showings, negotiations, and all other stages of the transaction.

Be Mindful of Fair Housing During Property Management
If you engage in property management, ensure your policies and practices align with fair housing laws. Screen tenants based on objective criteria such as income, rental history, and creditworthiness, rather than protected characteristics. Provide reasonable accommodation for tenants with disabilities, as required by law.

Compliance with fair housing laws is not just a legal obligation but an essential aspect of being a world-class real estate agent. By understanding and adhering to these laws, you demonstrate your commitment to professionalism, ethical conduct, and equal opportunity for all. Educate yourself, adopt a non-discriminatory mindset, and implement practical steps to ensure compliance. By doing so, you will not only protect yourself from legal consequences but also foster trust, credibility, and long-term success in your real estate career.

How do you handle legal disputes related to real estate transactions?

In the world of real estate, transactions can sometimes lead to legal disputes. As a world-class real estate agent, it is crucial to be prepared and equipped with the knowledge and skills to handle such situations effectively. In this question, we will explore the common legal disputes that arise in real estate transactions and provide you with a comprehensive guide on how to handle them professionally and ethically.

Understanding Common Legal Disputes
Legal disputes in real estate transactions can occur due to a variety of reasons, including contract breaches, misrepresentations, title issues, non-disclosure of defects, or disagreements over property boundaries. It is vital to have a thorough understanding of these potential disputes and be proactive in recognizing warning signs to minimize the risk of litigation.

Contract Breaches
One of the most common legal disputes arises from contract breaches. As a real estate agent, it is your responsibility to ensure that all parties involved

fully understand the terms and conditions of the contract. If a breach occurs, address the issue immediately to avoid further complications. Engage in open communication with all parties involved and attempt to negotiate a resolution that satisfies all parties. If a resolution cannot be reached, it may be necessary to seek legal advice or involve a mediator to resolve the dispute.

Misrepresentations and Non-Disclosure

Misrepresentations and non-disclosure of material facts can lead to legal disputes, especially when it comes to property defects or conditions. As a world-class real estate agent, it is imperative to maintain honesty and integrity throughout the transaction process. Provide accurate and complete information to clients, ensuring they are fully aware of any potential issues or risks associated with the property. If a dispute arises due to misrepresentation or non-disclosure, consult with legal counsel to understand the potential liabilities and take appropriate actions to resolve the dispute.

Title Issues

Title disputes can be complex and require a thorough understanding of property law. If a title issue arises, collaborate with a qualified real estate attorney to investigate and resolve the matter. Ensure that all necessary title searches and inspections are conducted to identify any potential problems early on. If a dispute occurs during the transaction process, it is crucial to involve all parties and work towards a solution that protects the interests of all involved.

Property Boundary Disputes

Disagreements over property boundaries can be contentious and require careful navigation. When faced with a boundary dispute, consult with a surveyor or a professional land use attorney to assess the situation. Gather all relevant documents, including surveys, deeds, and historical records, to determine the accurate property boundaries. Open communication and negotiation with the neighboring property owners can often lead to amicable resolutions. However, if a resolution cannot be reached, it may be necessary to pursue legal remedies to settle the dispute.

Handling Legal Disputes Professionally

When faced with a legal dispute, it is essential to handle the situation professionally and ethically. Here are some key steps to follow:

Communication: Maintain open lines of communication with all parties involved. Promptly address any concerns or disputes that arise during the transaction process.

Documentation: Keep detailed records of all communications, agreements, and transactions. These records can serve as valuable evidence if a legal dispute arises.

Seek Legal Advice: Consult with a qualified real estate attorney whenever a legal dispute arises. They can provide guidance and ensure that you are acting within the boundaries of the law.

Mediation and Arbitration: Consider alternative dispute resolution methods, such as mediation or arbitration, to resolve disputes amicably. These methods can save time, money, and preserve relationships.

Professionalism: Maintain professionalism and integrity throughout the dispute resolution process. Treat all parties involved with respect and work towards finding a fair and equitable resolution.

Handling legal disputes in real estate transactions requires a combination of legal knowledge, effective communication, and ethical conduct. By understanding the common legal disputes that arise and following the appropriate steps outlined in this question, you will be equipped to handle these situations professionally and ensure the best outcome for all parties involved. Your reputation and success depend on your ability to navigate these challenges with skill and integrity.

How well versed are you with the zoning and land use regulations?

As a world-class real estate agent, one of the key factors that sets you apart from the competition is your in-depth knowledge of zoning and land use regulations. Understanding these regulations is essential for successfully guiding buyers and sellers through the intricacies of real estate transactions. In this question, we will explore the importance of zoning and land use regulations, the different types of zoning, and strategies to stay well-versed in this ever-changing field.

The Importance of Zoning and Land Use Regulations
Zoning and land use regulations are the legal frameworks that determine how land can be used and developed within a specific jurisdiction. These

regulations are put in place by local governments to ensure orderly development, protect property values, and maintain the quality of life in a community. As a real estate agent, having a solid grasp of these regulations will enable you to provide accurate information to clients, identify potential issues, and offer valuable insights into a property's potential.

Types of Zoning

Zoning regulations typically divide land into different zones or districts, each with its own permitted uses, restrictions, and building requirements. The most common types of zoning include residential, commercial, industrial, and agricultural. Within these broad categories, there can be further subdivisions such as single-family residential, multi-family residential, retail, office, and manufacturing zones.

To become a world-class real estate agent, it is crucial to have a comprehensive understanding of the various zoning classifications in your area. Familiarize yourself with the zoning map of your jurisdiction and learn the specific regulations associated with each zone. This knowledge will empower you to advise clients on property usage, evaluate investment potential, and anticipate any challenges that may arise during the buying or selling process.

Staying Well-Versed in Zoning and Land Use Regulations

Study Local Regulations: Start by thoroughly studying your local zoning and land use regulations. Review the official zoning code, land use plans, and any amendments or updates. Familiarize yourself with the terminology, definitions, and processes involved. Attend workshops or seminars offered by local planning or zoning departments to deepen your understanding.

Network with Professionals

Connect with professionals involved in zoning and land use, such as planners, developers, architects, and land use attorneys. They can provide valuable insights and updates on current and upcoming zoning changes. Attend industry events and join professional organizations related to real estate and land use to expand your network and stay informed.

Monitor Zoning Changes

Zoning regulations are not static. Stay updated on any proposed or pending changes in your area. Regularly check local government websites, attend public hearings, and subscribe to newsletters or alerts from planning departments. Being aware of potential changes will allow you to advise clients accordingly and identify new opportunities.

Collaborate with Experts

When dealing with complex zoning issues, it is crucial to collaborate with professionals who specialize in zoning and land use. Develop relationships with experienced land use attorneys, zoning consultants, and environmental experts. Their expertise will help you navigate complex regulations and provide accurate guidance to clients.

Keep Learning

Zoning and land use regulations are constantly evolving. Commit to continuous learning and professional development in this field. Attend workshops, conferences, and webinars to stay up to date with the latest trends, case studies, and best practices. Consider pursuing certifications or advanced courses in zoning and land use to enhance your expertise.

Becoming a world-class real estate agent requires a deep understanding of zoning and land use regulations. By mastering these regulations, you can confidently guide clients through the complexities of property transactions, identify opportunities, and mitigate potential issues. Stay well-versed in local regulations, build a strong network of professionals, and commit to continuous learning. With this knowledge, you will set yourself apart as a trusted advisor and provide exceptional service to your clients.

How do you stay updated with changes in laws and regulations?

In the ever-evolving world of real estate, it is crucial to stay well-informed and up-to-date with the latest laws and regulations governing the industry. Being knowledgeable about changes in real estate laws not only ensures that you operate within legal boundaries but also helps you provide the best possible service to your clients. In this question, we will explore various effective strategies to stay updated with changes in real estate laws and regulations.

Join Professional Associations and Organizations

One of the most effective ways to stay informed about changes in real estate laws is to join professional associations and organizations. These entities often provide their members with regular updates and resources related to legal changes and updates in the industry. Take advantage of the wealth of information provided by these associations by actively participating in their events, workshops, and webinars. Additionally, many associations offer online platforms where you can access valuable resources, discussion forums, and legal updates.

Attend Continuing Education Courses

Continuing education is not only a requirement for maintaining your real estate license but also a fantastic opportunity to stay updated on changes in laws and regulations. Seek out continuing education courses that focus on legal aspects of real estate, as these courses are specifically designed to provide agents with the latest information on legal changes and how they impact their practice. By attending these courses, you can learn from experienced professionals and network with other agents who may have valuable insights into legal updates.

Engage in Online Research and Newsletters

The internet is a treasure trove of information, and it can be an excellent resource for staying updated on real estate laws and regulations. Subscribe to reputable real estate blogs, websites, and newsletters that cover legal aspects of the industry. These sources often publish articles and updates on new laws, court rulings, and regulatory changes. Additionally, consider following legal experts and real estate law firms on social media platforms like Twitter and LinkedIn, as they often share valuable insights and updates in real-time.

Network with Legal Professionals

Building relationships with legal professionals who specialize in real estate law can be immensely beneficial for staying updated with changes in the legal landscape. Attend local legal events, seminars, and conferences where you can meet attorneys who focus on real estate. Engaging in conversations with these professionals can provide you with valuable insights and help you understand the potential impacts of legal changes on your business. Moreover, establishing relationships with attorneys can be advantageous when you need legal advice or assistance in navigating complex legal issues.

Consult with Local Government Agencies

Local government agencies, such as city planning departments and housing authorities, are excellent sources for information on local laws and regulations. Reach out to these agencies and inquire about any recent changes or updates in real estate laws that may impact your area. Building a rapport with these agencies can also help you gain a better understanding of the direction in which local real estate regulations are headed, allowing you to better anticipate and adapt to future changes.

Collaborate with Peers

Networking and collaborating with fellow real estate professionals can be a powerful tool for staying updated on legal changes. Join local real estate investor clubs, attend industry conferences, and participate in online forums and discussion boards where you can interact with other agents. By engaging in conversations with your peers, you can exchange valuable information and insights about recent legal developments in the industry. Additionally, consider forming study groups with other agents to discuss and analyze legal cases and their implications together.

Consult with a Real Estate Attorney

In some cases, the best way to ensure you are fully informed about changes in real estate laws is to consult with a professional. Establishing a relationship with a real estate attorney can provide you with a dedicated resource who can help answer your questions, clarify legal issues, and keep you informed about the latest legal developments. While this may involve additional costs, the knowledge and peace of mind gained from having legal guidance can be invaluable in navigating real estate transactions.

Staying updated with changes in real estate laws and regulations is not a one-time effort but an ongoing process. Make it a habit to allocate time regularly to stay informed, and prioritize your professional development to maintain your standing as a world-class real estate agent. By continually expanding your knowledge base and adapting to legal changes, you will be well-equipped to provide the highest level of service to your clients while minimizing legal risks.

18 CRISIS MANAGEMENT

How would you handle a situation where a deal falls through at the last minute?

In the world of real estate, unexpected challenges are bound to arise, and one of the most disheartening experiences for any real estate agent is when a deal falls through at the last minute. However, it is important to remember that successful agents are not measured by the number of deals that close smoothly, but by their ability to handle setbacks and turn them into opportunities. In this question, we will delve into strategies and techniques to effectively handle situations where a deal seems destined to collapse. By mastering these skills, you will be well-equipped to safeguard your reputation, maintain client relationships, and even salvage deals that might otherwise be lost.

Maintain a Calm and Professional Demeanor
When faced with a deal falling through, it can be easy to let frustration or disappointment cloud your judgment. However, it is crucial to remain calm, composed, and professional throughout the process. Remember, your clients are relying on your expertise and guidance during this challenging time. By staying level-headed, you can assure them that you are in control of the situation and working diligently to find a solution.

Determine the Root Cause
To effectively address the situation, it is essential to identify the underlying reasons why the deal fell through. Was it due to financial issues, unexpected contingencies, or simply a change of heart by one of the parties involved? Understanding the root cause will help you develop a tailored strategy to resolve the issue.

Communicate Openly and Transparently

Strong communication is crucial in any real estate transaction, especially when handling a deal breakdown. Reach out to all parties involved and schedule a meeting to discuss the situation openly and transparently. Encourage each party to express their concerns, frustrations, and expectations. Actively listen to their perspectives and acknowledge their emotions to build trust and foster an environment where potential solutions can be explored.

Offer Alternative Solutions

Once you have a clear understanding of the issues at hand, brainstorm and propose alternative solutions to salvage the deal. For example, if financing is the problem, consider connecting the buyer with alternative lenders or exploring creative financing options. If the issue lies in contingencies, collaborate with the parties involved to find workable compromises. By presenting these alternatives, you demonstrate your commitment to finding a mutually beneficial resolution.

Consult with Experts

In complex situations, it can be beneficial to seek advice from experts in related fields. Engage with experienced real estate attorneys, mortgage brokers, or financial advisors who can provide insights and guidance. Their expertise may uncover options that were previously overlooked and help you navigate legal or financial obstacles that may arise.

Reassess and Adjust

If all efforts to salvage the deal prove unsuccessful, it may be necessary to reassess the situation and explore alternative paths forward. This could involve relisting the property, revisiting marketing strategies, or adjusting the asking price. It is vital to approach these decisions objectively, considering the market conditions, the property's unique selling points, and the client's objectives.

While a deal falling through at the last minute can be disheartening, it is an opportunity to demonstrate your resilience, adaptability, and problem-solving skills as a world-class real estate agent. By maintaining professionalism, open communication, and a proactive mindset, you can salvage failing deals, solidify client relationships, and set yourself apart in the industry. Think of every setback as an opportunity for growth and success.

How do you manage your business during a market downturn?

In the dynamic world of real estate, market fluctuations are inevitable. As a world-class real estate agent, you must be equipped to navigate the challenges that arise during a market downturn. While it can be a challenging period, it also presents a plethora of opportunities for those who adapt and strategize effectively. In this question, we will explore practical strategies and techniques to manage your business during a market downturn and emerge stronger than ever.

Assessing the Market Situation
The first step in managing your business during a market downturn is to thoroughly understand the current market situation. Study industry reports, analyze market data, and stay informed about economic indicators that influence the real estate market. By gaining insights into the specific reasons behind the downturn, you can better anticipate challenges and identify potential opportunities.

Diversify Your Client Base
During a market downturn, it is crucial to diversify your client base to minimize the impact of any one sector or market segment. Consider expanding your services to cater to different niches or demographics, such as first-time homebuyers, downsizers, or investors. By widening your target audience, you can increase your chances of maintaining a steady stream of clients even when certain segments of the market are affected.

Strengthen Your Network
Building and nurturing relationships is paramount in the real estate industry, particularly during a market downturn. Invest time and effort in strengthening your professional network by attending industry events, joining relevant associations, and actively engaging with fellow professionals. Collaborate with other agents, mortgage brokers, and contractors to develop a referral network that can generate leads and opportunities, even in challenging times.

Adapt Your Marketing Strategy
During a market downturn, your marketing strategy must be agile and adaptable. Consider reallocating your marketing budget to focus on cost-effective and targeted strategies. Leverage digital marketing techniques, such as search engine optimization (SEO), social media advertising, and email marketing, to reach a wider audience. Craft compelling content that

185

addresses the concerns and needs of potential clients during economic uncertainties. By adjusting your marketing efforts to align with the prevailing market conditions, you can remain relevant and attract potential clients.

Enhance Your Expertise and Skills

A market downturn provides an excellent opportunity to invest in your professional development. Utilize the extra time to enhance your expertise and skills. Attend industry seminars, take specialized real estate courses, or earn additional certifications to stay ahead of the competition. By continuously improving your knowledge and skills, you can position yourself as a trusted advisor and expert in your field, which can attract clients even during a market downturn.

Focus on Customer Service

During challenging times, maintaining exceptional customer service becomes even more critical. Nurture and prioritize your existing client relationships by offering personalized attention, timely communication, and valuable insights. Strive to exceed their expectations and provide exceptional service throughout the transaction process. Satisfied clients are more likely to refer you to their network, which can lead to new business opportunities.

Evaluate and Adjust Expenses

A market downturn necessitates a critical evaluation of your business expenses. Identify areas where you can reduce costs without compromising the quality of your services. Explore alternatives to expensive software or subscription services, negotiate better rates with vendors, and consider cost-sharing opportunities with colleagues. By optimizing your expenses, you can maintain profitability even during a challenging market environment.

Successfully managing your business during a market downturn requires adaptability, resilience, and a proactive approach. By assessing the market situation, diversifying your client base, strengthening your network, adapting your marketing strategy, enhancing your expertise, focusing on customer service, and evaluating expenses, you can navigate the challenges and emerge stronger from a market downturn. Embrace the opportunities for growth and development that arise during these periods, and you will position yourself as a world-class real estate agent capable of thriving in any market condition.

How do you deal with property damage or accidents during a showing?

As a top real estate agent, you will encounter various situations during showings, and unfortunately, property damage or accidents can sometimes occur. It is crucial to handle these situations with professionalism and efficiency to maintain your reputation and the trust of your clients. In this question, we will discuss strategies and best practices for handling property damage or accidents during a showing.

Preparation is Key
The first step in avoiding property damage or accidents is to be prepared. Before each showing, conduct a thorough inspection of the property to identify any potential hazards or areas of concern. Take note of any loose floorboards, faulty electrical systems, or other safety issues that could lead to accidents. Fix these issues or notify the property owner so they can be addressed before the showing.

Communicate with the Property Owner
Maintaining open lines of communication with the property owner is essential in handling property damage or accidents effectively. If you notice any damage or potential hazards during your inspection, inform the owner immediately. This demonstrates your professionalism and allows them to take appropriate action. Additionally, discuss any specific instructions or guidelines they may have regarding the property to further mitigate any potential risks.

Educate and Inform Prospective Buyers
During a showing, it is your responsibility to ensure that potential buyers are aware of any hazards or sensitive areas in the property. Clearly communicate any potential risks, such as uneven flooring, loose railings, or low-hanging fixtures. Encourage buyers to be cautious and to ask questions if they are unsure about anything. By setting clear expectations and educating buyers, you are minimizing the likelihood of accidents and property damage.

Supervise and Be Present
To prevent accidents and property damage during showings, it is crucial to be present and actively supervise potential buyers. While giving them space to explore, make yourself available to answer questions and provide

guidance. This will not only help ensure everyone's safety but will also allow you to address any concerns promptly. Be attentive to potential hazards and intervene if you notice any risky behavior, such as leaning on fragile surfaces or mishandling objects.

Take Immediate Action

In the unfortunate event that property damage or an accident occurs during a showing, it is vital to take immediate action. First and foremost, ensure the safety and well-being of all parties involved. If necessary, call emergency services or seek medical attention promptly. Once the immediate situation is under control, document the incident thoroughly, including photographs of the damage or accident scene, if applicable.

Communicate with all Relevant Parties

Following an accident or property damage, it is crucial to communicate with all relevant parties involved. This includes the property owner, the potential buyer, and any other individuals who may be affected. Notify the property owner about the incident, providing all necessary details and documentation. Offer your assistance in finding appropriate repair or restoration services if needed. Additionally, inform the potential buyer about the incident and any necessary steps they need to take, such as filing an insurance claim.

Mitigate Damages and Provide Solutions

As a world-class real estate agent, it is your duty to mitigate damages and provide solutions whenever possible. If the property damage is minor, consider involving professionals to repair or restore the affected areas promptly. If an accident occurred due to a property-related issue, such as faulty wiring, work with the property owner to rectify the problem and ensure it does not happen again. By actively taking steps to resolve the situation, you demonstrate your commitment to client satisfaction.

Dealing with property damage or accidents during a showing can be challenging, but by following these strategies and best practices, you can handle these situations with professionalism and efficiency. Remember always to prioritize safety, communicate effectively, and take prompt action. Your ability to handle such incidents effectively will not only protect your reputation but also inspire confidence in your clients, setting you apart as a world-class real estate agent.

How would you handle a client who is distressed about not being able to sell their property?

As a top real estate agent, you will inevitably encounter clients who are distressed about not being able to sell their property. This situation can be emotionally draining for both you and the client, but it is crucial to approach it with empathy, professionalism, and a problem-solving mindset. In this question, we will explore effective strategies to handle distressed clients, helping them navigate through their challenges while maintaining a positive and productive relationship.

Active Listening and Empathy

When a client is distressed about not being able to sell their property, it is essential to actively listen to their concerns and display genuine empathy. Remember, your role is not just about selling houses but also guiding and supporting your clients through the ups and downs of the real estate journey. Empathize with their frustrations and validate their feelings, showing that you understand the gravity of their situation.

Open and Honest Communication

Maintaining open and honest communication with distressed clients is crucial. Explain the current market conditions, any potential factors affecting the sale, and your professional opinion on the best course of action. Transparency is key in building trust and credibility with your clients, helping them make informed decisions.

Evaluate and Adjust Pricing Strategy

One of the most common reasons for a property not selling is an unrealistic price. Conduct a thorough evaluation of the market, comparable properties, and recent sales to determine if the listed price needs adjustment. Present your findings to the client, emphasizing the importance of pricing their property competitively. Collaboratively discuss a new pricing strategy that aligns with market trends and the client's goals.

Enhance Property Presentation

Assess the property's presentation and identify any potential improvements that could enhance its market appeal. A fresh coat of paint, decluttering, staging, or minor repairs can significantly increase the property's attractiveness to potential buyers. Collaborate with your client to create a plan for these improvements, highlighting their potential return on investment.

Innovative Marketing Techniques

If traditional marketing methods have not yielded the desired results, it may be time to explore innovative marketing techniques. Leverage technology and social media platforms to reach a wider audience. Utilize professional photography, virtual tours, and compelling property descriptions to captivate potential buyers. Consider hosting virtual open houses or webinars to showcase the property's unique features. Tailor your marketing approach to the target market, ensuring maximum exposure for the property.

Expand the Network

A well-established network is an invaluable asset when dealing with distressed clients. Reach out to your network of fellow agents, brokers, and industry professionals to explore alternative avenues for selling the property. Collaborate with colleagues who specialize in the client's property type or geographic area, pooling resources and knowledge to find potential buyers.

Provide Regular Updates and Feedback

During challenging times, it is crucial to maintain regular communication with your distressed clients. Provide them with updates on market trends, property showings, and any feedback received from potential buyers. This consistent communication demonstrates your commitment, builds trust, and keeps the client engaged and motivated.

Handling distressed clients who are struggling to sell their property requires a delicate balance of empathy, professionalism, and problem-solving skills. By actively listening, communicating openly, and implementing effective strategies like evaluating pricing, enhancing property presentation, and utilizing innovative marketing techniques, you can help your clients navigate through their challenges. The goal is not just to sell the property, but to provide support and guidance to your clients, fostering a long-lasting relationship built on trust and mutual success.

How would you manage your operations during an external crisis, like a pandemic?

In the face of an external crisis, such as a pandemic, real estate agents must adapt swiftly and strategically to ensure the safety of their clients, maintain business continuity, and even find opportunities amidst the challenges. This section will provide a comprehensive guide on how to manage your operations effectively during a crisis, with a particular focus on a pandemic like the one experienced globally in recent times.

Prioritize Safety and Communication

During a pandemic, the safety and well-being of your team, clients, and community should be your utmost priority. Stay informed about the latest updates and guidelines from health authorities and communicate them promptly to your team and clients. Establish a communication plan to keep everyone informed about any changes in operations, safety measures, and government regulations. Utilize various channels such as email, social media, and your website to disseminate information effectively.

Implement Remote Work Strategies

During a crisis, it is vital to embrace remote work strategies to maintain business continuity. Equip your team with the necessary tools and technology to work remotely, such as laptops, virtual meeting software, and project management tools. Establish clear guidelines and expectations for remote work, including setting regular check-ins and maintaining open lines of communication. Encourage your team to create a dedicated workspace at home and establish a routine to ensure productivity and work-life balance.

Leverage Technology

Technology plays a crucial role in managing operations during a crisis. Embrace online platforms and virtual tools to minimize in-person interactions while still providing excellent service. Utilize virtual tours, 3D walkthroughs, and high-quality photography to showcase properties remotely. Leverage video conferencing tools to conduct virtual meetings, consultations, and negotiations with clients. Implement digital document signing platforms to facilitate seamless transactions without physical paperwork. By embracing technology, you can continue serving clients effectively while adhering to social distancing guidelines.

Adapt Marketing Strategies

During a crisis, it is essential to adapt your marketing strategies to reflect the changing needs and priorities of your target audience. Focus on empathetic and informative content that addresses the concerns and challenges faced by clients during the crisis. Utilize social media platforms to engage with your audience, share valuable resources, and provide updates on the market and new listings. Consider exploring virtual events, webinars, or podcasts to stay connected with clients and showcase your expertise. By adapting your marketing strategies, you can build trust, maintain visibility, and even attract new clients during challenging times.

Cultivate Relationships and Provide Support

In times of crisis, real estate agents have a unique opportunity to showcase their commitment to their clients' well-being. Reach out to your existing clients to offer support, check on their needs, and provide guidance on navigating the market during uncertain times. Be empathetic, understanding, and flexible in accommodating their changing circumstances. Consider offering virtual consultations or hosting educational webinars to provide valuable insights to your clients. By cultivating relationships and providing support, you can strengthen your reputation as a trusted advisor and foster long-term loyalty.

Seek New Opportunities

While crises present numerous challenges, they also bring new opportunities. Stay vigilant and adapt your business model to identify emerging trends and shifts in the market. Explore alternative avenues such as property management, virtual staging, or investment counseling to diversify your income streams. Stay updated on government initiatives, grants, or assistance programs that could benefit your clients and position yourself as a knowledgeable resource. By embracing innovation and seeking new opportunities, you can not only survive but thrive during a crisis.

Managing operations during an external crisis, such as a pandemic, requires adaptability, resilience, and a customer-centric approach. By prioritizing safety, embracing technology, adapting marketing strategies, cultivating relationships, and seeking new opportunities, you can navigate the challenges of a crisis effectively. A crisis can be an opportunity for growth and innovation, and by implementing the strategies outlined in this section, you can position yourself as a world-class real estate agent even during the most challenging times.

19 SUSTAINABILITY AND GREEN REAL ESTATE

How knowledgeable are you about sustainable and green real estate?

In recent years, the real estate industry has witnessed a significant shift towards sustainability and green practices. As a world-class real estate agent, it is crucial to stay abreast of these changes and develop a deep understanding of sustainable and green real estate. This question aims to equip you with the knowledge and tools necessary to excel in this emerging field, allowing you to meet the demands of environmentally conscious clients and contribute to building a more sustainable future.

Understanding Sustainability
To begin our exploration of sustainable and green real estate, it is paramount to grasp the concept of sustainability itself. Sustainability refers to the practice of meeting present needs without compromising the ability of future generations to meet their own needs. In the context of real estate, this involves developing and maintaining properties that are environmentally responsible, socially equitable, and economically viable.

Key Principles of Sustainable Real Estate
Energy Efficiency: Energy-efficient buildings reduce their environmental impact by consuming fewer resources and emitting fewer greenhouse gases. Understanding energy-efficient design principles and technologies, such as insulation, high-efficiency HVAC systems, and energy-saving appliances, is crucial in assessing a property's sustainability.

Water Conservation: Conserving water is another essential element of sustainable real estate. Exploring ways to reduce water consumption through low-flow fixtures, rainwater harvesting systems, and drought-tolerant landscaping can greatly enhance a property's sustainability.

Green Building Materials: Being knowledgeable about various green building materials is essential as a real estate professional. These materials are sustainable alternatives to conventional ones and include recycled, reclaimed, or renewable resources. Familiarize yourself with certifications such as LEED (Leadership in Energy and Environmental Design) and their criteria for evaluating sustainable materials.

Indoor Air Quality: Sustainable real estate emphasizes creating healthy living spaces. Understanding the importance of indoor air quality and its impact on occupants' health is crucial. Knowledge of ventilation systems, air filtration, and non-toxic finishes will enable you to assess and promote properties that prioritize clean indoor environments.

Site Selection and Land Use: Sustainable real estate agents should consider the impact of property location and land use on the environment. Evaluating factors such as proximity to public transportation, walkability, and access to amenities can contribute to reducing carbon footprints and promoting sustainable living.

Green Certifications and Programs
One way to demonstrate your commitment to sustainable real estate is by becoming familiar with green certifications and programs. These certifications provide objective assessments of a property's environmental performance and can increase its value. The following are some of the most recognized certifications:

LEED (Leadership in Energy and Environmental Design): Developed by the U.S. Green Building Council, LEED is a globally recognized certification program. It assesses various aspects of a building's sustainability, such as energy efficiency, indoor environmental quality, and use of sustainable materials.

ENERGY STAR: ENERGY STAR is a voluntary program that certifies energy-efficient products, including appliances, windows, and HVAC systems. Understanding ENERGY STAR ratings and promoting ENERGY STAR-certified properties can enhance your credibility as a sustainable real estate agent.

Green Globes: Similar to LEED, Green Globes is a building certification program that evaluates a property's environmental impact. It provides a comprehensive assessment of sustainability performance and offers guidance on improving a building's efficiency.

Building a Sustainable Network

To excel in sustainable and green real estate, it is essential to build a network of professionals who share the same passion for environmental responsibility. Connect with local architects, contractors, and green building experts to expand your knowledge and collaborate on sustainable projects. Attend industry events, seminars, and webinars on sustainable practices to stay updated with the latest trends and technologies.

Becoming a world-class real estate agent requires a deep understanding of sustainable and green real estate practices. By embracing sustainability principles, familiarizing yourself with green certifications, and building a network of like-minded professionals, you can position yourself as an expert in this emerging field. As the demand for sustainable properties continues to grow, your knowledge and expertise will not only benefit your clients but also contribute to a more sustainable future for all.

How would you market a property with sustainable features?

In today's increasingly environmentally conscious world, properties with sustainable features are in high demand. As a world-class real estate agent, it is essential to understand how to effectively market such properties to attract the right buyers. In this question, we will explore strategies and techniques to showcase the sustainable features of a property, highlighting their benefits and appealing to eco-conscious buyers.

Highlight the Sustainable Features

When marketing a property with sustainable features, it is crucial to emphasize these aspects in your listing, advertisements, and promotional materials. Start by creating a comprehensive list of all the sustainable elements present in the property, such as energy-efficient appliances, solar panels, rainwater harvesting systems, low-flow fixtures, or smart home technology. Then, weave these features into your property descriptions, emphasizing the benefits they provide to potential buyers.

For instance, instead of simply stating that the property has solar panels, highlight how this feature reduces energy consumption and lowers utility bills. Focus on the long-term savings and environmental impact. By emphasizing these benefits, you can capture the attention of buyers who prioritize sustainability.

Leverage Visual Marketing

Visual marketing is a powerful tool when it comes to showcasing sustainable features. Use high-quality photographs and videos to capture the essence of these elements. For example, highlight a beautifully landscaped and water-efficient garden, or showcase the natural lighting and ventilation of a well-designed sustainable home.

Consider creating a virtual tour that specifically highlights the sustainable features of the property. This way, potential buyers can experience the benefits firsthand without physically visiting the property, which is especially valuable for international or out-of-town buyers.

Educate Buyers on Long-Term Cost Savings

Sustainable features often come with long-term cost savings, making them an attractive option for potential buyers. Educate your clients about these financial benefits to pique their interest. Provide them with data on potential savings from reduced utility bills, tax incentives for sustainable features, or government grants available for energy-efficient upgrades.

Create side-by-side comparisons demonstrating the financial advantages of a property with sustainable features versus a conventional property. By quantifying the long-term savings, you can help buyers understand the value proposition and make informed decisions.

Target Eco-Conscious Buyers

To effectively market a property with sustainable features, it is important to identify and target eco-conscious buyers. Utilize online platforms and social media channels that cater to environmentally conscious individuals. Engage with green living communities, sustainable lifestyle influencers, and platforms that promote eco-friendly practices.

Consider hosting or participating in local events related to sustainability, such as green fairs, energy efficiency workshops, or eco-home tours. This will not only help you connect with potential buyers but also establish your expertise in the sustainable real estate market.

Collaborate with Sustainable Experts

Collaborating with sustainable experts can add credibility to your marketing efforts and provide valuable insights to potential buyers. Partner with local environmental organizations, architects specializing in green design, or energy auditors to conduct assessments of the property's sustainable features. These experts can help identify potential improvements and provide certifications or ratings that authenticate the property's sustainability claims.

Marketing a property with sustainable features requires a strategic approach that highlights the benefits, educates buyers, and targets the right audience. By emphasizing the sustainable elements, leveraging visual marketing, educating buyers on long-term cost savings, targeting eco-conscious buyers, and collaborating with sustainable experts, you can effectively market these properties and attract the right buyers. The key is to showcase the value proposition of sustainability, appealing to both the environmental and financial motivations of potential buyers.

How do you advise clients on the cost and benefits of sustainable features in a property?

As a world-class real estate agent, one of your key responsibilities is to advise clients on the various aspects of a property, including its sustainable features. With the growing global concern for the environment and the increasing popularity of eco-friendly living, it is crucial to understand the cost and benefits associated with sustainable features. In this question, we will explore how to effectively assess and advise clients on the financial implications and advantages of sustainable features in a property.

Understanding Sustainable Features
Before delving into the cost and benefits, it is important to have a clear understanding of what sustainable features entail. Sustainable features refer to any design elements or technologies implemented in a property that reduce its environmental impact and enhance its efficiency. These features may include energy-efficient appliances, solar panels, low-flow plumbing fixtures, proper insulation, rainwater harvesting systems, and more.

Assessing the Cost:
Upfront Costs: The initial investment required to incorporate sustainable features can often be higher than traditional alternatives. As an agent, it is vital to help clients understand these upfront costs and guide them through the decision-making process. Collaborate with contractors and energy consultants to estimate the expenses accurately. It is essential to consider factors such as installation costs, equipment prices, and any necessary modifications to the property.

Long-term Savings: While the immediate costs may seem higher, it is crucial to emphasize the long-term savings associated with sustainable features. Educate your clients about the potential reductions in utility bills, maintenance expenses, and tax incentives available for eco-friendly properties. Discuss the payback period for the initial investment and highlight how the property's value can increase due to its sustainable features.

Return on Investment (ROI): Another aspect to consider when advising clients is the potential ROI of sustainable features. Research indicates that homes with energy-efficient features tend to have higher resale values and attract more potential buyers. By showcasing this information, you can help clients understand that the initial investment in sustainable features can result in financial gains when selling the property.

Evaluating the Benefits:
Environmental Impact: Highlight the positive environmental impact of sustainable features to clients who prioritize eco-conscious choices. Explain how these features reduce carbon emissions, conserve water resources, and contribute to a healthier, sustainable future. Appeal to their sense of responsibility towards the environment, as sustainable features align with their values.

Health and Comfort: Sustainable features often enhance the overall comfort and well-being of the property's occupants. Energy-efficient insulation, proper ventilation, and toxin-free materials create a healthier living environment, reducing the risk of respiratory issues and allergies. By emphasizing the improved indoor air quality and overall comfort, you can attract clients who prioritize their well-being.

Market Demand: Today's real estate market is witnessing an increasing demand for sustainable properties. Explain to your clients that by incorporating sustainable features, they are tapping into a growing market and attracting a broader range of potential buyers. Point out that many buyers are willing to pay a premium for eco-friendly properties, increasing the chances of a quicker sale.

Guiding the Decision-making Process
While assessing the cost and benefits is essential, guiding clients through the decision-making process is equally crucial. Here are a few strategies to assist your clients:

Tailored Approach: Understand your client's specific needs, preferences, and budget. By considering these factors, you can recommend sustainable features that align with their goals and financial capabilities. Avoid a one-size-fits-all approach and focus on providing personalized advice.

Clear Communication: Ensure that you communicate the cost and benefits of sustainable features in a clear and concise manner. Use visual aids, data, and case studies to support your explanations. This will enable your clients to make informed decisions based on accurate information.

Network and Expertise: Develop a network of professionals such as contractors, architects, and energy consultants who specialize in sustainable features. Collaborating with experts will enhance your credibility and assist in accurately assessing the cost and benefits for your clients.

When advising clients on the cost and benefits of sustainable features in a property, it is important to strike a balance between financial considerations and environmental responsibility. By providing a comprehensive understanding of the upfront costs, long-term savings, potential ROI, and various benefits associated with sustainable features, you can guide your clients towards making informed decisions. Sustainable features not only contribute to a greener future but also provide tangible financial and health benefits to the property owners.

How do you stay updated on the trends in sustainable and green real estate?

In today's rapidly changing real estate landscape, it is essential for world-class agents to stay informed about the latest trends in sustainable and green real estate. With increasing environmental concerns and an ever-growing demand for eco-friendly properties, being knowledgeable about sustainable practices will not only give you a competitive edge but also enable you to provide valuable guidance to your clients. In this question, we will explore various strategies and resources that will help you stay updated on sustainable and green real estate trends.

Attend Industry Conferences and Seminars
One of the most effective ways to stay informed about sustainable and green real estate trends is by attending industry conferences and seminars. These events provide a unique opportunity to learn from experts, network

with professionals, and gain insights into emerging sustainable practices. Look for conferences that specifically focus on green building, sustainability, or eco-friendly real estate. Notable conferences in this field include the Greenbuild International Conference and Expo, Urban Land Institute's (ULI) Spring and Fall Meetings, and the National Association of Realtors® (NAR) Green Designation Program. By actively participating in these events, you will be at the forefront of sustainable real estate practices, ensuring you are well-equipped to cater to the evolving needs of your clients.

Join Professional Associations and Groups
Another valuable resource for staying updated on sustainable and green real estate trends is to join professional associations and groups that focus on environmental sustainability. Organizations such as the U.S. Green Building Council (USGBC), Green Building Initiative (GBI), or the International Living Future Institute (ILFI) provide access to educational materials, industry research, and networking opportunities. By becoming a member, you can attend local question meetings, workshops, and webinars to gain insights from industry leaders. Additionally, consider joining online forums and LinkedIn groups dedicated to sustainable and green real estate. Engaging in discussions with like-minded professionals will allow you to exchange ideas, share experiences, and stay updated on the latest trends in the industry.

Follow Industry Publications and Blogs
Keeping abreast of sustainable and green real estate trends requires regular reading of industry publications and blogs. Subscribe to reputable magazines and journals, such as Green Builder Magazine, Environmental Building News, and Green Home Builder, which provide in-depth articles on sustainable building practices, energy efficiency, and eco-friendly design. Additionally, follow influential blogs and websites like Inhabitat, GreenBiz, and Treehugger, which highlight innovative sustainable projects and discuss emerging trends. Set aside dedicated time each week to read these publications and blogs, taking notes on key insights, case studies, and best practices. By staying well-informed, you will be able to provide your clients with accurate information and guidance regarding sustainable and green real estate options.

Continuous Education and Certifications
To truly excel in the realm of sustainable and green real estate, it is crucial to invest in continuous education and relevant certifications. Organizations like NAR offer specialized designations such as the Green Designation, which enhances your knowledge of green building principles, energy

efficiency, and sustainable practices. These programs provide comprehensive training, equipping you with the necessary skills to better serve eco-conscious clients. Additionally, consider pursuing certifications like LEED (Leadership in Energy and Environmental Design) or WELL AP (Accredited Professional) to deepen your understanding of sustainable building standards and healthy living environments. By acquiring these credentials, you demonstrate your commitment to sustainability and position yourself as a trusted advisor in the green real estate market.

Staying updated on sustainable and green real estate trends is a continuous journey that requires dedication and active engagement. By attending conferences, joining professional associations, following industry publications, and investing in continuous education, you will remain ahead of the curve, gaining a competitive advantage and providing exceptional value to your clients.

How do you consider sustainability factors when evaluating a property's value?

In today's world, sustainability has become a crucial consideration for individuals and businesses across various industries, including real estate. As a world-class real estate agent, it is imperative to understand and evaluate sustainability factors when determining a property's value. By incorporating sustainability into your evaluation process, you not only contribute to a better and greener future but also position yourself as an agent who fosters responsible investments. In this section, we will delve into the key aspects of sustainability and how they can impact a property's value.

Energy Efficiency
One of the primary sustainability factors to consider is energy efficiency. Properties that incorporate energy-efficient features such as solar panels, energy-efficient appliances, and proper insulation reduce energy consumption and, consequently, utility costs. These features directly contribute to the property's value by attracting environmentally conscious buyers who seek reduced energy expenses and a smaller carbon footprint.

When evaluating a property, assess its energy efficiency by reviewing its energy bills, insulation quality, HVAC systems, and the presence of renewable energy installations. Collaborate with energy auditors or consultants to conduct energy audits, providing potential buyers with detailed reports on the property's energy performance. Emphasize the long-term cost savings associated with energy-efficient properties to highlight their added value.

Water Conservation

Water scarcity and conservation have gained significant attention globally. Therefore, considering water-saving features and practices is crucial when evaluating a property's sustainability. Assess the property's water usage efficiency by reviewing its plumbing fixtures, irrigation systems, and the presence of rainwater harvesting or graywater recycling systems.

Properties equipped with low-flow fixtures, smart irrigation systems, and water recycling mechanisms are not only more environmentally friendly but also attract potential buyers who value sustainable living. Highlighting the property's water-saving features and potential savings on water bills can positively impact its value, particularly in regions prone to water scarcity.

Sustainable Materials and Construction

Another aspect to consider is the use of sustainable materials and construction practices. Sustainable materials, such as recycled or renewable materials, can significantly reduce a property's environmental impact. Evaluate the property's construction materials, insulation, and finishes to determine if sustainable alternatives have been utilized.

Furthermore, assess the property's overall construction quality, design, and orientation to ensure it maximizes natural light, ventilation, and energy efficiency. Properties that are built with sustainable materials and designed with a focus on environmental considerations tend to possess higher value due to their reduced ecological footprint and improved indoor comfort.

Location and Accessibility

The property's location and accessibility can significantly impact its sustainability and, consequently, its value. Consider properties that are in close proximity to public transportation, amenities, and services. Locations with excellent walkability and access to bike lanes promote sustainable transportation alternatives, reducing the reliance on private vehicles.

Additionally, evaluate the property's proximity to green spaces, parks, and recreational areas. Such amenities contribute to the overall sustainability and livability of the property, making it more appealing to potential buyers who prioritize a healthy and active lifestyle.

Certifications and Green Building Standards

Lastly, consider certifications and green building standards when evaluating a property's sustainability. Certifications like LEED (Leadership in Energy and Environmental Design) or ENERGY STAR demonstrate a property's adherence to specific sustainability criteria. These certifications provide tangible evidence of a property's value in terms of energy efficiency, water conservation, and overall environmental performance.

Familiarize yourself with the different certifications and their significance in the real estate market. If the property you're evaluating possesses any certifications, highlight them in your marketing materials and emphasize the added value they bring.

Incorporating sustainability factors into your evaluation process is vital to becoming a world-class real estate agent. By considering energy efficiency, water conservation, sustainable materials, location, and certifications, you can effectively assess a property's value from a sustainability perspective. This approach not only attracts environmentally conscious buyers but also positions you as an agent who values responsible and forward-thinking investments. Stay informed about the latest sustainability trends and technologies to provide the best guidance to your clients while contributing to a greener future.

20 INNOVATION AND THE FUTURE OF REAL ESTATE

How do you see the future of the real estate industry?

As a world-class real estate agent, it is crucial to stay ahead of the curve and anticipate the future trends and changes in the industry. The real estate landscape is constantly evolving, influenced by technological advancements, economic shifts, and changing consumer preferences. In this question, we will explore the future of the real estate industry and discuss the key trends and developments you need to be aware of to succeed in this ever-changing market.

Technology and Automation
One of the most significant factors shaping the future of the real estate industry is technology. Advancements in artificial intelligence, machine learning, and automation are revolutionizing the way business is conducted. In the coming years, we can expect to see an increasing reliance on technology to streamline processes, enhance efficiency, and provide personalized experiences for clients.

Virtual reality (VR) and augmented reality (AR) technologies will play a vital role in the real estate industry. These technologies will enable potential buyers to virtually tour properties, visualize renovations, and experience immersive showings. As a world-class real estate agent, it will be essential to embrace these technologies and leverage them to provide exceptional service to your clients.

Additionally, automation will simplify administrative tasks, allowing agents to focus more on building relationships and providing value to clients. From automated lead generation and management systems to AI-powered chatbots, agents will have more time to focus on high-value activities, such as negotiation and client engagement.

Sustainability and Green Living
Another trend that will shape the future of the real estate industry is the increasing emphasis on sustainability and green living. As environmental concerns grow, more buyers are seeking energy-efficient homes and sustainable living options. As a world-class real estate agent, it is crucial to familiarize yourself with green building practices, energy-saving technologies, and eco-friendly certifications.

Buyers will be looking for properties with features like solar panels, smart home automation for energy management, and sustainable materials. Being knowledgeable about these features and understanding the benefits they offer will give you a competitive edge in the market.

Furthermore, as consumers become more conscious of their environmental impact, neighborhoods and communities with a sustainable focus will gain popularity. Familiarize yourself with green initiatives and developments in your area, as this knowledge will help you match clients with properties that align with their values.

Changing Demographics and Preferences
Demographic shifts and changing consumer preferences are key drivers of change in the real estate industry. Understanding these shifts will allow you to adapt your strategies and cater to evolving market demands.

The millennial generation is becoming a dominant force in the homebuying market. Millennials value urban living, convenience, and experiences. They prefer walkable neighborhoods, access to public transportation, and proximity to amenities. As a world-class real estate agent, it is essential to understand their preferences and adapt your marketing and property selection accordingly.

Additionally, as the baby boomer generation enters retirement, there will be an increased demand for downsizing, age-friendly communities, and accessible living options. Become familiar with the concept of universal design and age-in-place features to meet the needs of this growing demographic.

Shift Towards Remote Work
The COVID-19 pandemic has accelerated the shift towards remote work, which will have a lasting impact on the real estate industry. With more companies adopting flexible work arrangements, buyers will have greater

freedom to choose where they live. This trend opens up new opportunities for agents to market properties in previously untapped areas.

Buyers may prioritize properties with dedicated office spaces, high-speed internet access, and proximity to coworking spaces. Understanding the needs of remote workers and being able to highlight these features will be crucial in attracting buyers in the future.

The real estate industry is on the cusp of significant transformation. Embracing technology, adopting sustainable practices, understanding changing demographics and preferences, and adapting to remote work trends are essential for becoming a world-class real estate agent.

As you navigate the future of the industry, always prioritize staying informed and continuously learning. Be open to incorporating new technologies, sustainable practices, and innovative strategies into your business. By doing so, you will position yourself for success and be prepared to thrive in the ever-evolving real estate landscape.

How do you incorporate innovative methods and strategies into your work?

In today's fast-paced and ever-evolving real estate market, it is essential for real estate agents to stay ahead of the game by incorporating innovative methods and strategies into their work. By embracing new technologies, thinking outside the box, and continuously adapting, you can position yourself as a world-class real estate agent, ready to tackle any challenge that comes your way. In this question, we will explore effective ways to incorporate innovation into your daily routine and elevate your success in the industry.

Embrace Technology
One of the most significant drivers of innovation in the real estate industry is technology. To stay competitive, you must fully embrace the technological tools available to you. Utilize customer relationship management (CRM) software to manage your contacts efficiently. Explore online platforms that provide virtual tours, drone photography, and 3D floor plans to enhance your property listings. Leverage social media platforms to market your properties and build a strong online presence. By leveraging technology effectively, you can streamline your processes, reach a

wider audience, and stay ahead of your competition.

Think Creatively

Innovation often stems from thinking outside the box. Challenge yourself to approach problems from different angles and find unique solutions. For instance, consider engaging with local artists to showcase their work in your open houses, creating a memorable experience for potential buyers. Explore partnerships with home staging professionals to create visually stunning listings that stand out from the competition. By thinking creatively, you can differentiate yourself and offer a fresh perspective to your clients, ultimately leading to increased success.

Continuous Learning

To incorporate innovative methods and strategies into your work, it is crucial to commit to continuous learning. Stay informed about the latest trends, market shifts, and emerging technologies in the real estate industry. Attend conferences, webinars, and workshops to expand your knowledge and network with other like-minded professionals. Consider joining professional associations and subscribing to industry-specific publications to stay up to date with the latest developments. By dedicating time to continuous learning, you can identify opportunities for innovation and ensure you remain at the forefront of your field.

Embrace Data-Driven Decision Making

Innovation in real estate is often driven by data. By harnessing the power of data analytics, you can make informed decisions and identify trends that will benefit your clients. Keep track of key market indicators, such as average home prices, days on market, and supply and demand ratios. Leverage online tools and platforms that provide real-time data to help you analyze market conditions and assist your clients in making well-informed decisions. By embracing data-driven decision making, you can provide a higher level of service, gain a competitive edge, and build trust with your clients.

Collaborate and Network

Innovation thrives in environments where ideas are shared, and collaboration is encouraged. Seek out opportunities to collaborate with other real estate agents, industry professionals, and even professionals from other fields. Attend networking events, engage in online forums, and participate in mastermind groups to foster connections and exchange ideas. By collaborating and networking, you can gain fresh perspectives, learn from others' experiences, and discover new approaches and strategies that can elevate your work.

Incorporating innovative methods and strategies into your work requires a commitment to embracing change and continuously evolving. By leveraging technology, thinking creatively, committing to continuous learning, embracing data-driven decision making, and collaborating with others, you can position yourself as a world-class real estate agent. Stay curious, be open to new ideas, and never stop pushing the boundaries of what is possible. Innovation is the key to staying ahead in today's dynamic real estate market.

How can virtual and augmented reality technologies be used in real estate?

In recent years, the real estate industry has been transformed by cutting-edge technologies like virtual reality (VR) and augmented reality (AR). These technologies have opened up a whole new world of possibilities for both real estate agents and prospective buyers. By incorporating VR and AR into their business strategies, world-class real estate agents can provide immersive experiences, streamline property viewings, and enhance the overall buying and selling process. In this question, we will explore the various ways in which virtual and augmented reality technologies can revolutionize the real estate industry.

The Power of Virtual Reality
Virtual reality has the ability to transport potential buyers into a property without physically being there. By putting on a VR headset, buyers can explore properties in a fully immersive and interactive environment. This technology offers several advantages:

Remote Property Tours
Virtual reality eliminates the need for buyers to travel long distances for property viewings. They can explore multiple properties from the comfort of their own homes, saving time and money. This is especially valuable for international buyers or those with busy schedules.

Enhanced Visualization
One of the biggest challenges in real estate is helping buyers visualize a property's potential. With VR, agents can create virtual staging by digitally furnishing and decorating empty spaces. This allows buyers to see the possibilities and imagine themselves living in the property, making it easier for them to make a decision.

Off-Plan Sales

For properties that are still under construction or in the planning stages, VR technology can be invaluable. Real estate agents can create virtual walkthroughs of these properties, giving buyers a realistic sense of the final product. This helps developers attract pre-sales and secure funding for their projects.

Augmented Reality Applications

While virtual reality creates a fully immersive experience, augmented reality enhances the real world by overlaying digital information onto physical spaces. Here's how AR can be utilized in real estate:

Property Visualization

Augmented reality allows buyers to view detailed property information simply by pointing their smartphones or tablets at a property. This technology can display property specifications, historical data, and even pricing information. It provides buyers with instant access to crucial information, empowering them to make informed decisions.

Virtual Staging

Similar to VR, AR can be used for virtual staging. Instead of needing a VR headset, buyers can use their smartphones or tablets to visualize how a property would look with different furniture arrangements or color schemes. This technology saves time and money by eliminating the need for physical staging.

Real-Time Property Tours

AR can transform property viewings by overlaying digital information on physical spaces. Buyers can use their devices to see additional details about a property, such as room dimensions, nearby amenities, or even potential renovation options. This real-time information enhances the buyer's understanding of the property and helps them envision their future in it.

Virtual and augmented reality technologies have the potential to revolutionize the real estate industry. By embracing these innovations, world-class real estate agents can provide immersive experiences, streamline property viewings, and enhance the overall buying and selling process. Through virtual reality, buyers can remotely explore properties and visualize their potential, while augmented reality empowers them with real-time information during property tours. As these technologies continue to evolve, they will undoubtedly become integral tools for real estate professionals striving to provide exceptional service and stand out in a competitive market.

How does the growth of smart homes affect the real estate industry?

In recent years, technological advancements have revolutionized various industries, and real estate is no exception. One of the most significant developments is the emergence of smart homes. With the integration of advanced technologies into residential properties, smart homes have become a sought-after feature for homebuyers. As a world-class real estate agent, it is crucial to understand how the growth of smart homes affects the industry and adapt accordingly to meet the changing needs and demands of clients.

Enhanced Property Value
Smart homes offer a range of features that enhance property value. Home automation systems allow homeowners to control various aspects of their homes remotely, such as security systems, lighting, temperature, and even appliances. These technological conveniences not only increase comfort and convenience but also appeal to potential buyers seeking homes with advanced features. Consequently, properties equipped with smart home technology often command higher prices and attract a broader market segment, resulting in increased profitability for real estate agents.

Increased Market Demand
With the proliferation of smart devices and their integration into everyday life, the demand for smart homes has surged. Homebuyers are now more inclined to invest in properties that offer the latest technological advancements. As a real estate agent, it is essential to recognize this growing trend and adapt marketing strategies accordingly. Highlighting the smart features of a property in listings, staging homes to showcase their technology capabilities, and leveraging social media platforms to target tech-savvy buyers are effective methods for attracting potential clients.

Energy Efficiency and Cost Savings
Smart homes are renowned for their energy-efficient features, which resonate with environmentally conscious buyers. Integration of smart thermostats, energy monitoring systems, and smart lighting allows homeowners to optimize energy usage, leading to reduced utility bills. Consequently, energy-efficient smart homes appeal to a broader market

segment concerned with sustainability and cost savings. As a real estate agent, it is crucial to emphasize the long-term value of energy-efficient features when marketing smart homes, as they can be a significant selling point for potential buyers.

Enhanced Security and Safety

One of the most compelling advantages of smart homes is the enhanced security and safety they offer. From smart locks and security cameras to advanced alarm systems, homeowners can remotely monitor and control their properties, providing peace of mind. Additionally, smart homes can integrate fire and leak detection systems, offering an extra layer of safety. Understanding the security and safety benefits of smart homes is vital for real estate agents, as it allows them to effectively communicate these advantages to potential buyers, especially those with families or concerns about home security.

Potential Challenges and Considerations

While smart homes offer numerous benefits, it is essential to acknowledge potential challenges and considerations. The rapid pace of technological advancements means that smart home technology can quickly become outdated. As a real estate agent, it is crucial to stay updated on the latest advancements and educate buyers on the potential need for future upgrades or replacements. Additionally, privacy concerns may arise due to the integration of smart devices into homes. Educating clients on data security measures and ensuring they understand the implications of interconnected devices is essential for building trust and maintaining client satisfaction.

The growth of smart homes has had a profound impact on the real estate industry. From increased property value and market demand to enhanced energy efficiency and security, smart homes have become a sought-after feature for homebuyers. As a world-class real estate agent, it is essential to adapt to these changes and effectively market smart homes to meet the evolving needs and preferences of clients. By understanding the advantages, potential challenges, and considerations associated with smart homes, real estate agents can position themselves as knowledgeable professionals in the ever-changing landscape of the industry.

How do you adapt to changing buyer preferences in real estate?

As a top real estate agent, one of the key skills you must possess is the ability to adapt to changing consumer preferences and technological advancements in the industry. The real estate landscape is constantly evolving, driven by the ever-changing needs and expectations of consumers as well as the rapid advancements in technology. In this question, we will explore strategies and techniques to help you stay ahead of the curve and effectively adapt to these changes.

Understanding Changing Buyer Preferences

Consumer preferences play a significant role in shaping the real estate market. To adapt to these changes, it is crucial to stay informed about the latest trends and understand what drives these preferences.

Here are a few strategies to help you adapt:

Stay informed: Subscribe to industry newsletters, attend conferences, and engage in professional networking to stay updated on the latest trends and consumer preferences. This knowledge will help you anticipate shifts in the market and adapt your strategies accordingly.

Market research: Conduct regular market research to identify the changing needs and preferences of your target audience. This can be done through surveys, focus groups, or analyzing market data. By understanding your clients' preferences, you can tailor your services to meet their specific requirements.

Embrace diversity: The real estate market is becoming increasingly diverse. To adapt, it is essential to understand and appreciate the unique needs and preferences of different demographic groups. By offering personalized services that cater to diverse clientele, you can gain a competitive edge.

Leveraging Technological Advancements: Technological advancements have revolutionized the real estate industry, providing agents with tools and platforms to streamline their processes and enhance their services. To adapt to these advancements, consider the following strategies:

Embrace digital marketing: In today's digital age, a strong online presence is crucial. Utilize social media platforms, create a professional website, and optimize your content for search engines. Digital marketing allows you to reach a wider audience and showcase your expertise, ultimately attracting more clients.

Harness the power of data: Big data analytics can provide valuable insights into market trends, client preferences, and pricing strategies. By leveraging data-driven tools and platforms, you can make informed decisions, predict market shifts, and offer tailored recommendations to clients.

Virtual tours and 3D visualization: With the rise of virtual reality and 3D visualization technologies, you can offer clients immersive virtual tours of properties without them physically being present. This not only saves time but also allows clients to visualize themselves in the space, leading to more informed decision-making.

Collaborate with proptech companies: Proptech (property technology) companies are constantly developing innovative solutions for the real estate industry. Collaborate with these companies to leverage their technologies and stay ahead of the competition. Whether it's using AI-powered chatbots for customer support or employing blockchain for secure transactions, proptech can enhance your services.

Continuous learning: To adapt to technological advancements, it is crucial to continuously update your skills and knowledge. Attend workshops, webinars, and training sessions to stay abreast of the latest technologies and learn how to incorporate them into your business practices.

Adapting to changing consumer preferences and technological advancements is an ongoing process in the real estate industry. By staying informed about consumer trends, embracing diversity, and leveraging technological tools, you can position yourself as a world-class real estate agent. The key is to be proactive, willing to learn, and open to embracing new strategies and technologies that will help you thrive in this ever-evolving industry.

What role do you see AI and machine learning playing in the future of real estate?

In recent years, the real estate industry has witnessed a rapid evolution driven by advancements in artificial intelligence (AI) and machine learning. These technologies have the potential to revolutionize how real estate agents operate, improving efficiency, accuracy, and customer experience. In this section, we will explore the role AI and machine learning play in reshaping the future of real estate and how aspiring agents can leverage these technologies to become world-class professionals.

Enhanced Data Analysis
One of the most significant impacts of AI and machine learning in real

estate is their ability to process vast amounts of data quickly and accurately. With the right tools, agents can access comprehensive market data, analyze trends, and make informed decisions in real-time. AI algorithms can identify patterns and predict market fluctuations, helping agents provide clients with valuable insights. By leveraging these technologies, real estate agents can offer a competitive advantage by delivering data-driven advice and recommendations.

Improved Customer Experience
AI-powered chatbots and virtual assistants have become increasingly prevalent in the real estate industry, enhancing the customer experience. These virtual agents can handle initial inquiries, schedule property viewings, and provide essential property details, freeing up agents' time for higher-value tasks. Additionally, AI algorithms can analyze customer preferences, helping agents curate personalized property suggestions, ultimately improving customer satisfaction and loyalty.

Efficiency and Automation
AI and machine learning can automate time-consuming tasks, streamlining processes and enhancing efficiency for real estate agents. For instance, AI-powered software can automatically process and sort property listings, matching them with buyer preferences, saving agents valuable time in searching for suitable options. Machine learning algorithms can also automate paperwork, contract generation, and document management, reducing errors and minimizing administrative burdens. By embracing automation, agents can focus more on building relationships, negotiating deals, and providing personalized services.

Predictive Analytics for Pricing and Investment
AI and machine learning algorithms have the potential to revolutionize property pricing and investment analysis. These technologies can consider numerous factors, such as location, market trends, historical data, and property attributes, to generate accurate property valuations. With this information, agents can provide clients with precise pricing suggestions, aiding in negotiations and ensuring fair deals. Moreover, AI can assist investors by identifying promising opportunities based on historical data, real-time market trends, and financial indicators. By leveraging predictive analytics, agents can offer clients valuable insights, adding substantial value to their services.

Virtual and Augmented Reality
Another groundbreaking application of AI and machine learning in real estate is the integration of virtual and augmented reality (VR/AR)

technologies. These immersive experiences allow clients to virtually tour properties, giving them a realistic sense of the space without physical visits. AI algorithms can enhance VR/AR experiences by providing interactive features, such as customizing room layouts, changing interior designs, or virtually staging properties. This technology not only saves time for both agents and clients but also expands the reach of property listings, attracting international buyers and investors.

The role of AI and machine learning in the future of real estate is undeniable. These technologies have the potential to transform how real estate agents operate, improving efficiency, accuracy, and customer experience. By embracing AI-powered data analysis, automation, predictive analytics, and VR/AR technologies, real estate agents can position themselves as world-class professionals, offering unparalleled services to clients. To stay ahead in an ever-evolving industry, it is crucial for aspiring agents to embrace these transformative technologies and adapt to the changing landscape of real estate.

How do you leverage technology in your work as a real estate agent?

In this digital age, technology has become an indispensable tool for real estate agents to enhance their productivity, efficiency, and overall success. With the advancement of technology, agents have access to a vast array of resources that can streamline their workflow, improve communication with clients, and stay ahead in a highly competitive industry. You can leverage technology to elevate your career and become a world-class professional.

Online Presence and Marketing
Establishing a strong online presence is crucial in today's digital landscape. Utilize social media platforms, such as Facebook, Instagram, and LinkedIn, to showcase your listings, share valuable content, and engage with potential clients. Create a professional website that highlights your expertise, provides an easy way for clients to reach you, and showcases your listings effectively. Leverage search engine optimization techniques to ensure your website is easily discoverable by potential clients searching for real estate in your area.

Virtual Tours and 3D Visualization
One of the most significant advancements in real estate technology is the ability to create virtual tours and 3D visualizations. These tools allow

potential buyers to explore properties remotely, saving time and effort for both you and your clients. Invest in professional photography, videography, and virtual tour software to create immersive experiences that bring your listings to life. By offering virtual tours, you can attract a larger pool of potential buyers and generate higher-quality leads.

Customer Relationship Management (CRM) Systems

Effective communication and organization are key to success in real estate. Implementing a CRM system will help you manage client relationships, track leads, and automate certain aspects of your workflow. These systems allow you to store client information, schedule follow-ups, and track interactions. With built-in automation features, you can send personalized emails, reminders, and market updates, ensuring you stay top-of-mind with your clients.

Mobile Apps and Tools

The real estate industry is fast-paced, and being able to access information on the go is essential. There are numerous mobile apps designed specifically for real estate agents to streamline their tasks and enhance productivity. Some apps provide access to multiple listing services (MLS), allowing you to search for properties, pull up detailed information, and share listings with clients instantly. Others offer e-signature capabilities, enabling you to sign contracts digitally, saving time and reducing paperwork.

Data and Analytics

Harnessing the power of data and analytics can provide valuable insights into market trends, pricing strategies, and client behavior. Utilize tools such as Zillow, Redfin, or Realtor.com to access comprehensive market data, including recent sales, median prices, and neighborhood statistics. Understanding these trends can help you make informed decisions when advising clients and negotiating deals. Additionally, using analytics tools, such as Google Analytics, can help you track website traffic, monitor the performance of your online marketing efforts, and make data-driven adjustments to your strategies.

Online Document Management

Gone are the days of printing and physically signing stacks of paperwork. Online document management systems, such as DocuSign or HelloSign, allow you to send, receive, and sign documents digitally. This not only saves time and money but also provides an eco-friendlier approach to your business practices. These systems offer secure and legally binding electronic signatures, ensuring the integrity and validity of your contracts.

Leveraging technology is essential in becoming a world-class real estate agent. By establishing a strong online presence, embracing virtual tours and 3D visualization, implementing CRM systems, utilizing mobile apps and tools, leveraging data and analytics, and adopting online document management, you can enhance your productivity, streamline your workflow, and provide exceptional service to your clients. Embrace technology as a powerful ally and stay ahead of the competition in the ever-evolving real estate industry.

CONCLUSION

Congratulations on completing your journey through this comprehensive guide on becoming a world-class real estate agent! As you close this final chapter, you stand at the threshold of an incredibly exciting and dynamic career path. The knowledge and skills you've acquired from each chapter are not just theoretical; they are the keys to unlocking your full potential in the world of real estate.

Embarking on this career, you are not just a salesperson; you are a trusted advisor, a neighborhood expert, and a key player in some of the most significant decisions of your clients' lives. The real estate market is ever-evolving, brimming with opportunities and challenges that will test your skills, resilience, and adaptability.

Remember, your success in this field is not solely measured by the number of sales you make, but by the relationships you build, the trust you earn, and the impact you have on your clients' lives. Your ability to listen, empathize, negotiate, and stay ahead of market trends will set you apart as a top-tier real estate agent.

Stay committed to continuous learning and self-improvement. The landscape of real estate is constantly changing, and so should your strategies and approaches. Network with other professionals, keep abreast of the latest industry developments, and never underestimate the power of innovative marketing.

As you step into the world of real estate, armed with the insights and strategies from this book, you are more than prepared to rise to greatness. Your journey might be filled with unexpected turns, but remember that each experience is a stepping stone to mastering your craft.

Celebrate this moment, for you are about to embark on one of the most rewarding and fulfilling careers. Your dedication and hard work have brought you here, and now, the real adventure begins. Embrace the challenges, cherish the victories, and above all, stay passionate about helping people find their perfect home or investment. Here's to your success as a world-class real estate agent!

www.ingramcontent.com/pod-product-compliance
Lightning Source LLC
Chambersburg PA
CBHW071154290526
45796CB00007B/43